Women Speak

Volume Seven

Edited by Kari Gunter-Seymour

Spoken Word and Fine Art Selections

WOMEN OF APPALACHIA PROJECT™

Acknowledgments:

Appalachian Heritage, Appalachian Journal, Artemis, Arts & Letters, Balance of Five, Change Seven, Clinch Mountain Review, Coming of Age, Escape Into Life, Indolent Books' What Rough Beast Series, LexPoMo Anthology 2019, Malpais Review, New Limestone Review, New Southerner Literary Magazine, ONE ART, Pegasus, Pluck! The Journal of Affrilachian Arts & Culture, Quiet Diamonds, Red Eft Review, Shadows on Wood, Sow's Ear, Still: The Journal, Streetlight Magazine, Sweet Tree Review, SWIMM, The Fourth River, The Locust Years, Wellspring

ISBN: 978-1-7354002-8-0
Sheila-Na-Gig Editions
Russell, KY
www.sheilanagigblog.com

EDITOR: Kari Gunter-Seymour
LINE EDITOR: Kristine Williams
COVER DESIGN: Kari Gunter-Seymour
COVER ART: *Singing Sisters,* AngelynDeBord

INQUIRIES:
Kari Gunter-Seymour, Executive Director
womenofappalachia@gmail.com
www.womenofappalachia.com
FACEBOOK: Women of Appalachia Project

Women Speak

Contents

"…toward all the uncertainty that lies ahead,
a wild song beating in her chest." – Laura Sweeny

In Memoriam

Susan Sheppard
July 1, 1955 – April 19, 2021

Wabash in the Alleghenies

I come from a place where
Coon-dogs drag their chains
Like beggars rattling a tin cup,
Where mountain twilight smokes
Like an old woman on a stoop.
I come from a place where cows
Turn sad, sublime faces toward passing cars
As we dream of escaping fenced in meadows,
Where clots of blackberries sweeten
The edges of the woods and sate
Our pangs of hunger. I come from
A place where lye soap and hog bones
Float up in dingy bucket water,
Where the rinsed sunlight of
A steadied heaven never reaches
The deepest hollers. Where I come
From broken stars hide like thieves
Inside the dark boughs of cedar,
And icy waters rush over
The dam like widow's hair.

(from *Women Speak*, Volume Five)

Introduction

Dear Reader:

Within these pages you will find remarkable fine art and a lavish mix of Appalachian female voices – northern, central, southern, Affrilachian, Indigenous, Asian-Appalachian, LGBTQ, those with disabilities and developmental differences, emerging and well established – every one stepping up to speak the truth of Appalachia. Poetry, story, song, essay, memoir each a tribute to Appalachian endurance, honor, courage, love of family, community and the land; providing evidence of how even against the odds we continue to thrive and stand strong in our convictions, working together to build awareness and overcome marginalization and stereotype, our words and rich heritage our catalyst.

The first year, the Women of Appalachia Project (WOAP) consisted of five women fine artists from Athens County, OH, who exhibited their art along with four poets who presented a reading in honor of Women's History Month, events sponsored and hosted by Ohio University's Multicultural Center. Roll forward 13 years. Today the Women of Appalachia Project™ is a non-profit 501(c)3 and holds trademark rights to the name. The "Women Speak" anthology is celebrating its seventh volume. Hundreds of women have participated from throughout nearly every Appalachian state as well as out-migraters with strong Appalachian roots. The WOAP Facebook page has 42,000 friends from all over the world. We perform our work at colleges, major libraries and galleries throughout OH, WV and KY.

The success of this organization is based on the work of every single woman who does, has or will someday take part, whether as a participant, volunteer, partner or supporter. We are a thriving network, a sisterhood in every sense of the word, working toward the same goal – to lift up Appalachia and showcase it in all its magnificent glory. No need for extreme acts, protest signs or marches. The work speaks for itself:

"… the salty sweet citrus-sting of those hills and hollers,
all the meanings of the words *broken* and *blessed* and *kin"* —Lisa Parker

Oh, reader! Prepare your heart.

Kari Gunter-Seymour
Founder/Executive Director
Women of Appalachia Project™

Ellis Elliot

Rusted Nails and Rat Bones

What are these letters from Daniel
but earnest spells he cast for us,
like a valley veiled in fog of well-meant
wishes, and how do I tell him there is
much more to fear than rebels in our hills?

Children escaped my body like blackbirds,
wide-jawed and hungry, I sought
anything we could find to eat, filled apron pockets
heavy with persimmons and pokeweed.
Dan, Jr.'s foot got pierced through by a barn nail.

I packed a poultice of sumac and sweetgum,
and prayed for it to work, like the jug
of pennyroyal tea Granny Grills brought.
After Daniel's last stay, I gulped it bitter
without sugar, let it gush down my chin
and soak my chest. I begged the Lord's forgiveness,
asked mercy for my intent, to prevent
another suckling mouth at my breast.

What is our nest made of but rusted nails
and rat bones in the woodpile, half-empty
cookpots and equal parts yearning and dread?
I wring my bloodied rags at creek side, flutters
hushed in my heaving belly as I weep.

Ellis Elliot

Unseen

(Granny Grills)

Sometimes I can't find God in the scrawl
of blue mountains around me, try as I might to pull
a bucket of sense from the well of the earth
to pour floods on the fires of war

in the blue mountains around me, I might pull
bulbs to brew, chant verses, conjure storms
that pour, then flood. The fires of war
roll from the hills into homes, women holler

for my bulbs to brew, chant verses, conjure storms
as balm for raw palms, light to drink the darkness
rolling from hills into homes, women holler
over sickbeds, small coffins, mothers

are balm for raw palms, light that drinks darkness,
buckets of sense from the well of the earth.
Mothers holler over sickbeds, small coffins,
and sometimes I can't find God in the scrawl

Kari Gunter-Seymour

The House, The Barn, The Sheep, The Chickens

Problem was, she felt too much
or not at all, a practiced yearning
that had no name. Her kids grown,
gone, forty years behind her,
fields rutted, shutters slumping,
the barn propped and cock-eyed,
all those young bride prayers wasted.

Creatures like sheep, used to traveling,
know about moving on, guided by
the compass of their will, boredom
a kind of armor, desire a grassy knob
worth dying for. How utterly
a body is overruled by heartache,
an affliction that can't be outrun.

Outside red oaks thrash, tangled
in root and bird song and whatever
might fall from the sky.
Her last undoing was to set her sassy
banties free to peck and roam,
scratch out a destiny of their own.

Kari Gunter-Seymour

Bone Thin

Sunday morning, the alarm set
for dawn, I gargle lemon water
to loosen phlegm, open vocal cords.
Mother postured at the piano, paces me
up and down the major scales,
Are you washed in the blood of the lamb?

I dress in a starched white blouse,
an A-line skirt hemmed precisely
below the knee. Mother stands behind me
in the mirror– cat eye glasses, Pentecostal bun
– hot-curls my *ragged mane into
a semblance of respectable.*

Later, in the choir loft, mother leans,
her coffee breath all over me,
whispers loud enough
for the soprano section to hear,
You're too pretty to be so fat.

CJ Farnsworth

Severstal Re-Opens the Yorkville Plant in Time for Christmas

My father worked, when he wasn't laid off
for Wheeling-Pittsburgh Steel.

He wrapped leftovers in silver paper and carried his Char-Vac
Stanley full and hot and promised, once, to take me

inside his crane cab 100 feet up to see the mammoth fires
and molten steel. One time, while opening a can of corn

he showed me how his knuckles were becoming calcified
and cyclopean, then made me listen to Joe Cocker and Janis Joplin

and once a Shakespeare play and another time his buddy (he always
had a buddy doing this or that) sing *Knock, Knock, Knocking*

On Heaven's Door. We listened to that knock, knock, knocking
for months riding along Route 2, at night, when the mills were lit

like wedding halls or fairy forests, thousands of gold lights raining
and bursting in and out of the river – all the while, machines

pressing ingots forcing impurities to the top – machines that roared
and raged below my father who sat on an inflatable orthopedic donut

…walking through a hotel lobby in Naples last December, a man brushed
my arm with his newspaper and it became that bright and hot.

CJ Farnsworth

Thumb Finding Test

All I can do is find a sunny hillside,
(if I could not?) a hillside in the sun.
And I do. It's all I can do—sit

on this sunny grassy sloping patch
tapping each thumb on the woken grass.
The sun is silent from where I sit
and the hill itself is too eminent to utter.

A breeze attends. I feel it under my hat,
a hat that smells like my head—smokey,
composty, a hint of black strap molasses
perhaps. The hill slides into a lake.

A swan carries two children, but there
is nothing of dreams beneath this hill
nothing of myth—a value-added
to the stretch. Squirrels (does it matter

what color?) on tenterhooks cross
against the light, crouch and descend
headfirst from this tree to that, claws
a swivet, coming right up to scratch.

Now that the season has changed
my indehiscent brain conceives only
the occupation of acorn foraging
or momming oodles of blind offspring.

I drove behind an Amish horse and buggy
to arrive hillside, but there is a hillbilly
exhaust in the distance. As well, this hill face
gets sun all the long day and this reality

paints a portrait of destructive lust. Why
does sitting on a hillside in the sun
feel so much like work? Like all I can do?
Why do I feel like distant hillbilly exhaust?

Perhaps it is being so dull, such a cheap
sketch, desiderating myself into this frame
onto this canvas of au courant, raw light
that mimics pulling pillars on the retreat.

Randi Ward

Mountain

What
is there
to say
when
you can
never
quite
get out
of your
own
way?

Randi Ward

Trough

Ten deer
and
two horses
drink
from this
trough,
but the frog
never leaves.

Randi Ward

Daisy

Forgive
my being
cruel—
if you're left
to guess,
you already
know
the truth.

Sherrell Wigal

January Alone

Across Pine Lane, afternoon,
dark in its winter cloak,
nuzzles the tethered brown goat,
stretching his neck,
toward what foliage
is left on the still green shrub.
Only hunger swings the pendulum
between here and there
as long shadows
shutter what is left of light.

At four o'clock
waxing gibbous moon
hangs in the bluest sky this year,
promises yet another bright night.
Crows circle and glide
in an almost setting sun.
Cadence of melting snow
thrums an ancient rhythm
heard only by those
alone this day.

Over the frozen valley
early evening
becomes silvered vein of water
as the James River
moves toward tomorrow
sings its own liquid song,
certain as sorrow
of its own destination.
Where will this river go
when no one is watching?

Sherrell Wigal

Say I Was a Poet

After I die,
prop the bones
of a beautiful bird
in my mouth.

Call a medicine woman
back from my home star.
Offer tobacco, cedar, sage, sweet grass,
the seven silent petitions of passage.

For all these words are only feathers
from the dark hollow of my throat.
Plumes which wait for a wing,
a way to lift,   rise,   fly.

To soar from my lips,
fingers, to become
a prayer of fire
hitching a ride homeward.

Elaine Fowler Palencia

The Sweetest Girls

Bless their hearts, they are the sweetest girls you could ever hope to meet, but sometimes you just wonder why people turn out the way they do. Donna Jean Preston and Holly Maggard have been friends since they were two. As you may know, they were both in "the class the stars fell on" at Tolliver School. Out of that one class of thirty kids we got a doctor, an engineer at NASA, a judge, two professors, a lawyer, a high school principal, and the point guard on the team that took Blue Valley College to the NIT. To this day, you'll find plenty of people who say those two are the smartest of the lot. They're still the only ones from here that ever placed in the top ten at the Kentucky State Math Tournament. Egging each other on. That was the key.

Definitely as a librarian I saw it. They were the readingest girls. Donna Jean would get obsessed with Beethoven, or how to make silk, or dogs in the White House, and read everything she could find on it. She'd become an expert on whatever it was. It's a wonder she didn't get scoliosis in the fourth grade from lugging around *Gone with the Wind*, which she read every bit of it. Holly was just the opposite—she'd read a little bit on every subject. She'd read the label on a couch cushion if she didn't have anything else to read. She always wanted to know about more things than Donna Jean did. They reminded me of the hymn, "Deep and Wide," Donna Jean being deep in her knowledge and Holly being wide.

When they were in the fifth grade, Mrs. Fraley was going through the change and couldn't hardly cope. So she turned the remedial reading part of her class over to them. They'd take the slow kids in the back room and put them through their paces. I don't reckon my nephew Harlan would ever have learned to read without them.

In high school Donna Jean dated Crozier Moffett. They made a nice couple, both tall and dark-haired and studious, but it was just a convenience for both of them, so they'd have a date for prom and such; he never allowed her to wear his letter jacket.

Holly gave her folks more trouble: she dated some pure-T rascals. Jane had to take her to Bradenton one summer to get shed of Bobby Wasson, which it took him six years to get out of high school. You couldn't turn your back on that boy. He's a policeman in Detroit now and look what happened there.

Anyway, Holly and Donna Jean were valedictorian and salutatorian. Holly went to UK and Donna Jean went to Centre. After graduation Donna Jean got a fellowship to study English literature at the University of Chicago. Holly interviewed with SunTrust and was offered a big job in

Atlanta, with opportunities to advance.

The next thing we heard was that Donna Jean was involved with one of her married professors. Merle Wilson ran into them at the Field Museum when she was up there chaperoning the band. Merle tried to catch her eye but Donna Jean just looked straight through her. Merle said the old boy was wrinkled up like a Shar-pei.

So that was Donna Jean. Meanwhile Holly was climbing the ladder at SunTrust. Every so often she'd come home and go to DAR and Book Club with her mother. Wore her hair awfully short and these mannish suits, which made some people talk. Then she up and married a man from somewhere in Central Europe. He did something with computers, don't ask me what.

They got married real quick in Atlanta, so didn't anybody from here get to go to the wedding. Pretty soon she had what we used to call a seven-month baby. Of course, anymore that kind of thing doesn't matter. Nowadays my niece Madison wouldn't have to marry that sorry Elkins boy, which I could just drive red-hot railroad spikes through his eyes for the way he's treated her.

Donna Jean ended up teaching in Michigan. The old professor left his wife and went with her. Turned out that Donna Jean was his fourth, all of them his students. When one got too old, he'd trade down for a younger one.

I believe Donna Jean and Holly lost touch there for a while. Donna was raising a couple of that old coot's children from his third marriage and Holly was working seventy-hour weeks at SunTrust.

Then Donna Jean's mother, Clotilde, got breast cancer. Donna being an only child, there wasn't any question. So she took a leave of absence and came home to take care of her mama, and that's how we found out the old coot had left her for somebody else. I guess he thought he had one more run in him.

Pretty soon their class's fifteenth year reunion came along. Holly came in for that, and it was while the group was sitting around the pool at the Comfort Inn about two in the morning, that she got to talking to Dave Goble.

Now, Dave's a good old boy, but he's nowhere near Holly's level. His people are from over around Cropsey and none of them ever went past high school, if that far. One old bachelor uncle lived in a tree, I swear to God. Great huge hollowed out trunk, old growth and big enough to stable a team of horses in. I've seen pictures.

Be that as it may, that very night Holly and Dave ran off together. When she told her husband that the reunion really didn't last ten days and that she'd gone to Myrtle Beach with Dave, he left out for his country, taking the boy. So that's been going on for years, trying to get little Ethan back.

Meanwhile, Clotilde died; she was stage four by the time she was diagnosed. Donna Jean's daddy retired from selling insurance and went back to Knott County, where he has a little farm. He's growing heirloom vegetables, they say, and teaching about them in the local foodways program.

Donna Jean stayed on here. She lives in the family home on Wilson and teaches AP English at the county high school. Everybody—students, faculty, and Mrs. King, the principal—is terrified of her. She's a wonderful teacher, but she'd as soon pinch your head off and throw it out the window as look at you. At school, that is. In civilian life, she'd do anything for you.

About a year ago a boy brought a gun to school and was showing it around in her homeroom. Donna Jean hit him upside the head with the Webster's Collegiate Dictionary and took it away from him. She keeps an actual print dictionary on her desk to show the kids how handy they are. His family sued the school district for loss of hearing in the ear she clobbered and won a pile of money, which they blew gambling at Tunica, but she wasn't charged.

Several years ago, she adopted a little girl from Guatemala that she named Rosalee. Cutest child, those big old black eyes full of mischief.

Holly and Dave live in the Ox Branch neighborhood. Her parents retired to Florida. She and Dave have two boys and Holly works at the hospital. Dave works for the telephone company like his daddy did. He's a good provider, but if he was to have an idea, he'd take out his squirrel gun and shoot it.

Every Friday afternoon after school, Donna Jean drops by Holly's. Holly works four days a week on flextime, so she's home on Fridays. They're still great readers, but both of them turned down invitations to be in the Book Club, which you can't get in unless you're a legacy like Holly, whose mother belonged, or a spot opens up when somebody dies. This is unheard of. Nobody else in the ninety-year history of the Club has ever turned down membership.

Holly and Donna Jean have their own book club, just the two of them on Friday afternoons, drinking coffee and discussing what they've read. Some of us wonder if they ever talk about how they ended up back here. I mean, lots of people manage to escape from Blue Valley. Nowadays half the kids end up in Lexington or Atlanta. Why couldn't these two stay escaped, our brightest stars? Not that this isn't the best place in the world to live.

Anyway, here's what happens every Friday afternoon. Holly will have baked a Milky Way Cake or some other gooey dessert, which they sample, and then she'll send half of it home with Donna Jean. Donna's face is still thin and she still has her waist, but over the years she's gotten right pear-shaped. She'll protest, but then Holly will say, "Oh, take it to Rosalee, God love her," and Donna Jean will relent.

Now, on the way over there from school, Donna Jean will have stopped at the Donut Shop and gotten six regular glazed and six blueberry cake donuts, supposedly for Holly's family, although sometimes it's crullers.

As soon as Donna Jean leaves, Holly will open the donut bag and inhale to the bottom of her lungs. She was stocky to begin with, muscled like a pit bull, and she can barely keep her figure by going to Curves every day before work. So after she's inhaled, she'll take that bag of donuts out to the garbage can and throw it in, opening the bag so the donuts fall unprotected onto the other garbage. I've got an eyewitness to that.

Meanwhile, Donna Jean is walking home with the Milky Way Cake or the chess pie or the dozen chocolate frosted brownies. At the corner of Haggan Park is a public waste can, which she will throw the dessert in. Did I say Holly always double-wraps it in plastic wrap and aluminum foil? Then Donna Jean walks on home, her mind afire with thoughts of triumphing over Holly. You can see it, the way her face lights up. But she regrets letting go of all that comfort and pleasure. So, she rounds up Rosalee from Mrs. Johnson, who's been watching her, and they drive out to McDonald's for a #1 Big Mac meal, then to Dairy Queen for Peanut Butter Buster Parfaits. It's their Friday routine. Rosalee is fattening up like a shoat.

Meanwhile, Holly is thinking about the sugar and fat she sent home with Donna Jean. She can't eat the part she's kept, because she owes that to Dave and the boys. But one time, taking a walk to resist temptation, she accidentally saw Donna Jean throw half of her homemade cheesecake into the garbage can at the park. So now, every week, Holly waits a couple of minutes after Donna Jean leaves, then goes to the park and retrieves the dessert she's just given her, which is wrapped so carefully to keep out germs. Then she goes home, shuts herself in the bedroom, and eats it. On Saturdays, they both try to work it off on the college track. Donna Jean goes jogging around seven a.m. Holly's there later, maybe around ten.

One time I asked my husband why they go through this rigmarole.

"I guess it gives them relief," he said.

"What do you mean, relief?"

"Well, maybe like me going fishing."

"But relief from what?"

He shrugged.

"And by the way, mister, what do *you* need relief from?" I asked.

But he'd gotten up from his recliner and was on his way to the garage, where his boat is. I'm surprised I got that much out of him.

Corie Neumayer
Girl With Owls

Marguerite Floyd

River Blues

Somebody must have taught you how to play the blues. It must have been down by the river in that old bar and grill, the one with the little neon sign flashing as if it were still 1951 and the women still paused to check their seams before following their dates inside the darkness for the best $3.95 T-bone dinner in the entire dirty city, where the waitresses called you "Sugar," and always brought you the whiskey neat.

Later, the singer in sequins would hold her head high, auburn hair like fire in the smokey lights, the only woman you ever knew who could wear true red on her mouth. And when she sang the timbre of her voice slipped its tongue up your spine like a promise that things would never end. And you believed. As surely as the river's current pulled at the shore, you believed.

You can't sing the blues in this city today, this place of twisted streets that forget their own name and fork around one another like the small fear that curls in your mind when you're lost. A closed-in town like a picture on a postcard you find in a shoebox from so long ago you no longer remember who sent it, no longer understand the scrawled "Thinking of you" in faded ballpoint blue.

And there's no river here, no sound of waters like faith moving beneath the silly city noises, no barges calling out in the afternoons. Yet you still measure your life against each clear note rising out of her throat as if she goes on singing forever, even though she's probably dead now, or married to some merchant who sells heavy metal sheet music, later counting his little profits like reciting lessons from a grammar book, never hearing the river call like Jesus after the damned.

Mary Ann Honaker

Hometown

If you drive far enough, the four lane
ends abruptly in a bulldozed heap
of fresh turned dirt and broken limbs.

Turn right and you can descend
into a coal camp where tight packed
company shacks are mostly

still inhabited, curtains in windows,
plastic chairs on porches, laundry
swaying in cluttered backyards.

Further still and blasted peaks
of a strip-mined giant glisten nudely
in fog-damped air, ghosts

rising in wispy clumps up slopes.
Crammed in a narrow valley
is a town from the fifties:

houses of brick and cut stone so close
you could reach out your window
to knock on your neighbor's wall.

A red-bricked downtown, some stores
still open, others boarded over,
a single restaurant, a single gas station.

The streets are empty. Someone scoops
the town up in a sheet, lifts the corners,
ready to close it. That's how tall, how close,

how sharp the mountains are.
Fountain after fountain ripples, gleams
down the walls of the canyon

cut to make a road.
I return home, my face splashed
and awakened by awe, washed clean.

*

My neighbors sit on the shaded porch
again, while a red sunset quietly burns.
The talk today is of a man near my age,

whose son has taken his prized
convertible Mustang. No one knows
if he'll ever see it again. They'll take

checks from your mailbox, tools
from your shed. Do you have an alarm?
You should have cameras. How much

are cameras? Last week the kid took
the groceries back to Walmart for cash,
was gone for days. He's into it bad.

Once Howard was offered a blow job
in the automotive department. Betty's kid
is on drugs too, and Howard's stepson.

*

When I was a kid I'd take off
on my bike and ride for miles.
Stop by a roadside store

to buy Pixie Stix and Baby Ruth
bars, Fun Dip and Fireballs.
On weekends we'd picnic in the park,

our only worry a profusion of gnats
and fat black ants. Yesterday a woman
was raped by two men on a bike path.

*

I like to walk along the rooftop
of the Gorge, peer down into that cut,
watch the hawks circle the sun.

But they tell me not to go alone.

I'm more afraid here than just outside
of Boston; I double-lock the doors,
don't sit on the porch after dark.
Every day the landscape dips me
in beauty. What has happened here.

*

Help Wanted signs in every window.
No one can find a worker who's clean.
At night crickets thrum and thrum,

by day shrill buzz of cicadas.
Sometimes I swerve when driving,
stunned silly by roadside wildflowers.

A dirty dog is chained in a driveway.
He barks and barks. No one speaks to him
but to scold him. I want to steal him,

give him a bath, let him lounge
in my bed. A short walk from here,
you can step from the road

onto a beaten path through trees.
There's firepits and boxes with blankets
in them, discarded dirty clothes.

Bottles everywhere: cheap wine,
liquor, diluted and bitter
brands of beer. I try to make a line

in my mind, pile mountains
and flowers and hawks on one side,
misery and filth on the other.

Mary Ann Honaker

We Have Become Death

A patch of forest remains between this house
and the next, where a doe often hides with her fawn.
Crows circumscribe it all day, screeching out

to hallow the shadows of hewed trees.
I knew a clergyman whose life tasted so bitter
he hung a birdfeeder in a pruned maple,

sat with a sour sting in his throat
until the crows came; then he shot them.
But I don't mind their cawing, a raw sound

that matches my heart, which I scraped out
as one would a pumpkin, carved it a snarl,
set the inside on fire. At night the black birds

recede into their black nests to rest in the black trees
against the black sky and are silent. Somewhere the man
coughs up his cud of hate and masticates it, savoring.

I can't know what a crow knows: if a wind is weak
and will drop me, spiraling; or if it has lift
lively enough to sky all the heaviness of me.

My candle burns lower, weeping wax, and finally
the wick gives up its stench of endings. Maybe crows
do long for the once-forest that is my house, midnight lit,

as I long for my heart before I cored and monstered it,
even for the glow that blackened its walls. I am charred.
An owl I cannot see croons her three funerary notes.

Mary Ann Honaker

Violin

A violin may have a sound teased
out of it the color of reeds. It may wail
like a reed would if it were your heart,
bending in a winter blast, it may sound

like a wedge of dark stabbed
into a chest, as if night were a knife
and it were pruning free an apple's core—
if that pith were your heart.

A violin may sound like a blue updraft
of summer wind that lifts a bruised leaf
broken free too soon of its source,
unhinged and lilting upward

awash in sunlight, pierced through
by it, as it never was before
in the company of its fellows, in the shadows
of its fellows. A violin could sound

like all these things walking down
a path together, a path mapped meticulously
by some sovereign hand, some knowing
hand, it can sound held warmly

against a throat, a pulse tocking
quietly, insistently, into its hollow—
a void like the void where the stars churn—
it can sound planned, created

but created like the stars were,
by a brilliant burst from some crammed
and overwrought thing, expanded into
nothingness, and making it mean.

Cecile Dixon

Bill Withers

July 4, 1938-Slab Fork, WV
March 30, 2020-Los Angeles, CA

On the day that Bill Withers gained his wings social media held a wake for him. My feed overflowed with his photos and YouTube versions of his many songs. The articles gave his age as eighty-two. Surely, he couldn't be that old. Then I sighed, remembering that I was now sixty-one myself. Bill Withers' song lyrics had played a large role in a turning point in my life. It wasn't a good point and I didn't choose the right road. I scrolled the Internet until I found "Lean On Me" and clicked the link.

The now familiar, clear, simple keyboard notes filled me with melancholy for my squandered youth. I'd been a troubled thirteen-year-old when I'd first heard this song. My divorced parents both had remarried within months of their separation and since the time of Cinderella, step kids haven't been popular. Cute little kids might blend in, but nobody wanted a hormonal, greasy long- haired, hippie want-to-be, mouthy thirteen-year-old girl around. Basically, I'd become homeless.

I was feeling particularly forsaken and outcast one evening as everyone had left and I was alone. A friend of my mother's phoned. (I'll call him PE.) PE and I chatted, each of us complaining about how shitty my mother had treated us. He asked if I wanted to go for a ride. I said "sure" even though I knew there'd be hell to pay if I got caught. The only time anyone seemed to acknowledge my existence was when I broke one of their commandments.

PE picked me up in his midnight black, sixty-eight, Thunderbird. Just sitting on the real leather, bucket seats made me feel special and lightened my mood a little. We didn't talk much. Just listened to the radio. This car had FM stereo and picked up stations from Lexington and even Cincinnati, with just a little static. We listened to Steppenwolf, CCR and Otis Redding. He drank beer and smoked a joint, offering both to me. I refused and stuck to smoking the Marlboros I kept hidden under the torn liner of my fringed purse.

PE was good looking, older than me, but much younger than my mother. He had money, or at least his parents did. He had a car. To my young mind, this was the most wonderful thing ever. He could leave this backward, Kentucky town anytime he wanted to. Maybe he'd take me with him. Maybe, if we had sex. The excitement and fear of sex was ever present in my mind. It always swirled around all the good and bad.

As he drove I watched his bearded, profile in the red glow of the dashboard lights. I was young and inexperienced, but I thought I knew

37

about men. I knew that sometime before this night was over, he'd want to have sex. His reason would be payment for giving me a ride, or to get even with my mom, or maybe it was because he was young and male. At thirteen I didn't know or understand these reasons, but my outcome was the same. If we had sex, I'd feel dirty and bad. I'd be a whore just like the preacher and my daddy said. A whore, just like my mama.

For hours we drove in and out of town, up the strip where people sat on the hoods of their parked cars and waved. I felt grown up and proud to be out, alone with a popular guy. PE drove through the town's two traffic lights, then back out into the country, around the winding mountain roads. The darkness beyond the car's headlights was like thick velvet. Bugs flew through the open windows and tangled in my hair. I didn't care. I felt free and I wanted the feeling to go on forever.

When the simple, opening notes of "Lean On Me" came on the radio, they seemed to mirror my mood. I'd never heard the song before, but PE had. He knew the words and sang along. When the tempo picked up he drummed the rhythm on the steering wheel with his fingertips.

The lyrics to the song voiced my emotions in a way that my adolescent brain could never find words for. Bill Withers wrote this song for me. The song expressed the things I couldn't say but felt so much. I wanted someone to lean on, to listen to me, to care about me. I wanted to matter.

The song was winding down when the blue lights of a police car strobed behind us. "Fuck," PE said as he shoved his baggie of weed under the seat and pulled to the curb.

My heart pounded. Would I go to prison because he had weed? Through the side mirror I watched as a tall policeman got out of the patrol car. He walked to the passenger side and straight to my door. From his belt he pulled out a flashlight and shone it in my face. The haunting refrain of the song's ending two words played.

"Your mom's worried about you," the uniformed officer said as I blinked at the bright light. Without another word he opened the passenger door and roughly pulled me out of the car. I tried to resist by hitting with my fist, but he was stronger.

I glanced at PE. He sat with both hands glued to the steering wheel, staring straight ahead. "Call me," I pleaded. Withers repeated the same two words fourteen times. PE didn't even look my way.

The policeman dragged me across the gravel and shoved me into the back of the cruiser. "My mom," I spat, "'ain't worried about me, she's just worried that people might say what a sorry mother she is. That's all she cares about, what people think."

"Don't matter, either way you're going home."

He had said home. Part of me was relieved, but another part, that rebellious part wanted to add jail to my list of experiences. Within six months I'd be married. My list of new experiences grew every day, every minute.

Mr. Bill Withers was right about one thing. There's always tomorrow. Until there isn't.

Mary Beth Whitley
Field Study

Anne Dyer Stuart

The Daughter

And he might tell you, as you cross over
railroad tracks near the blues' birthplace, nothing
out here but ragweed and concrete, heat now
beginning to pull you under, about

the daughter who cut up her mother
with gardening shears. Each time you drive through
neighborhoods along the creek he'll point out
a different house. Half listen to fires

in the middle of the night, Peeping Toms
everybody knows, sawed-off shotguns,
secrets dug up like bones. You imagine
she got out of prison alone, shut

the front door. Footsteps plush in carpet
vacuumed twenty years ago. Town's
beating heart outside her window.
Table set: bones of the favorite cat

beside the stove. But the clothes, what fit?
Mirror above the dresser—black raisins
pressed in the dough of her face. Who
are you, if not the things you've done?

Anne Dyer Stuart

Kindergarten, St. James Parish

We are kindergartners, our knees expose
us, vulnerable light bulbs, fried gooey eggs.
That one will lose her parents in a murder-
suicide in nine years. This one will turn
her daddy's gun on herself in seven
after her parents find her in bed
with a boy. One she'd grown up with right next
door. One she'd been brave enough to love.

And the girl to her right?
Bully at the white supremacist school,
taunted the girl ashamed of her body,
her parents, that boy they'd caught her with
in bed. She'd tried to hang herself first.
Called her friend and told her it didn't work.

There's the refrigerator box I kept
my secrets in, whispered them to the girl
who lost her parents, until some boy heard
me tell her I liked him and hurled
a baseball at my head. Seven years
later Daddy will take me out of school
for the funeral, make me a peanut
butter and banana sandwich, better
than the kind you make for yourself, and
in the backyard cicadas will sing, raw
shells of themselves tossed across the lawn.

Anne Dyer Stuart

Lake Chico County Fair

I.

At Lake Chico County Fair, a girl
with the body of a woman, one
I wouldn't have twenty years later,

jiggled in pale flesh, shiny white heels.
Already she had woman problems: cysts
on her ovaries, a six-foot tall

mother with platinum hair. Little girl,
I was still, so short sometimes I could
disappear, already starving, ashamed
of my gymnast flesh.

II.

Grandmother scared me with tales of murder,
the girl decapitated in her own
convertible, one who drove right under

a truck. Or the girl who plucked herself deaf
with a Q-tip. She had the nerve to do
two things at once. Grandmother's daddy

lost his head in a logging accident.
Men called his family to the scene. At five
years old Grandmother walked over

to him, what was left of her father.
It's a Presbyterian God, one who's
already made up his mind. Shot you out

like a stone at a window, like the thirty-
three panes my brother broke as a kid. You're
a girl burning for some nameless want,
a girl punished for wanting it.

Donna Weems

Ballad of The Lady of the Wood (Song)

I met a maiden in the wood
  A reckoning in me stirred
Her eyes searched mine long questioning
  She said not a word

Beholding and transfixed with awe
  I knew no one could claim her
Her beauty so ephemeral
  Yet she was no stranger

Her hair was bound in bunting blue
  Her dress in buttonwood flowers
Shoulders draped with a lacy cape
  Made from virgin's bower

There was magic in her movements
  Like a shimmering of the leaves
Clear eyes like pools reflecting
  Beneath the willow tree

I entered a world more perfect
  Than I could ever create
Its beauty was in the abundance
  Of life in its native state

I could not reach out to touch her
  For I knew she would disappear
I stood rooted and unmoving
  In hope and in fear

The lady of the wood came to me
  In fullness before me stood
Her presence instilled a yearning
  To linger as long as I could

She pressed her body into mine
  The dam released a flood
My soles grew shoots into the Earth
  Sunlight bathed my bursting buds

I met a maiden in the wood
  A reckoning in me stirred

Donna Weems

Waters Rising (Song)

Mount Port Crayon's deep in clouds
Listen, the waters sing out loud
Red spruce forest steeped in snow
The soil brims with overflow

Water seeps through grass and moss
From under logs and cracks in rocks
Once a gully now a streambed
The mountain is its watershed

Refrain:
Waters are rising arise from your bed
Waters are rising clear your head
Join the chorus when the pitch is found
When singing together voices resound

Spruce Run spills over wooded banks
Rushing past rocks and soil dank
Once a trickle, now deep and strong
Rapids thunder in valleys long

The mountains echo the full voice roar
Red Creek's rising upon its shore
Rolling rocks and bending trees
Winter's thaw has set Red Creek free

Refrain

Red Creek, Dry Fork, Blackwater Falls
Black Fork, Shavers, nothing forestalls
Waters gathering from their source
The mighty Cheat's raging voice

Refrain

Lois Spencer

Lily

Lily appeared in our fifth grade class the first day back after Christmas break. When Miss Brothers attempted to introduce her, Lily turned beet red and buried her face in the skinny arms folded on her desk. Neatly braided pigtails fell on either side of a body that looked brittle enough to break. A lot of eye-rolling passed around the classroom and a few giggles, but Miss Brothers quashed it with a look and went on with class like nothing had happened.

During recess, Lily stayed at her desk while the rest of us bundled into coats and boots. Groups of comrades huddled amid piles of dingy snow shriveling toward oblivion, and Stevie and I wandered over to the swings and kicked at the ice in the wells beneath. An old soul possessed of a keen, imaginative mind, Stevie never worried about fitting in while I hated being a misfit. But my dad had a spotty work history and stood out among the bevy of fathers who worked themselves into early graves, and Mom and I lived with the consequences. None of that mattered to Stevie any more than my being a girl. Recess was nearly over when I finally asked for his take on Lily's reaction that morning.

One of Stevie's passions was watching black and white WWII movies, so his answer shouldn't have surprised me: "Could be something like shell shock."

I stopped kicking and stared at him. "And how many fifth grade girls have you seen in a war?"

Stevie's wide gray eyes were fixed on a batch of snow clouds amassing in the west. "You don't have to be in a war for bad things to happen."

My feet had grown as frozen as the ice we'd been kicking, so I went inside ahead of the bell. In the classroom I found Lily at her desk, her surprisingly blue eyes staring through one of the tall windows into the dark winter day. From the adjoining cloak room I heard voices—Miss Brothers' flute-like, Mr. Sellers' so deep it reverberated inside the narrow, hook-lined space. Something told me they were discussing Lily.

Miss Brothers' head popped around the open door. "You're early, Missy. Is something wrong?"

"My feet got cold."

She gestured me in, and I caught a faint scent of moth balls as the principal's wool suit passed close to my nose. Alone with Miss Brothers, I wanted to ask her about Lily, but I feared she would think I'd been eavesdropping.

* * *

That afternoon, half-numb from cold, I rushed into the living room. Mom had just added a log to the fireplace and was positioning it with the poker, cigarette held steady in her teeth. Sparks shot up from the bed of red coals as though intent on escaping through the chimney, some sacrificing their freedom to ignite tiny outcroppings on the new log where smaller branches had once sprouted. I tossed my coat aside and plopped into a wide upholstered rocker. Mom returned the poker to its stand and knelt to loosen my boot latches ahead of my stiff, reddened fingers.

When my boots were dripping on the hearth, she scooted me over and joined me in the rocker, her warmth hastening my thaw. The combined scents of tobacco, Castile soap, and wood smoke assured me I was home, and home had always meant safety. But Stevie's comment about Lily, along with my own musings, had teased open a worrisome thought: Was something bad, worse than what I'd learned to tolerate, waiting for me?

During the summer harvest, my great-uncle Hank showed up routinely with produce from his garden. Tomatoes and green beans we couldn't use up right then Mom cold-packed in Mason jars for winter. When the weather grew cold, he brought wood for the fireplace and cook-stove and sometimes side-meat after butchering. When he came bearing gifts, Mom always offered him a cup of coffee and a slice of whatever she had baked, even if he often was, as she put it, three sheets in the wind. She could slip the cup and plate onto the table in front of him and skirt away without a pause. But I was never quick enough. Uncle Hank's moist, insistent hand would pull me to his side as he demanded "a little bit of sugar." The hand released me only after I had kissed the whiskery cheek. The worst part was feeling that a pair of red-rimmed eyes clouded with alcohol could see right through every stitch I had on. While Mom never intervened, she never left me alone with him either. She knew something I didn't, and whatever it was put me on high alert.

* * *

February's lacy snowflakes and milder temperatures came as a relief. So did the fact that Lily no longer panicked if Miss Brothers laid a hand on her shoulder. When Valentine's Day drew near, I dragged out last year's shoebox and re-covered it with paper hearts a lot neater than the ones I tore off; I had learned to fold the paper before cutting so the sides of the hearts matched. Everybody showed up with a mailbox and valentines on the big day except Lily. Just as if she'd been expecting Lily to need them, Miss Brothers produced a box, red wrapping paper, and an extra package of cards. Watching the two heads bent together over their work brought a sudden tightness to my throat and stinging to my eyes. Glancing at Stevie, I caught him observing the tableau also.

Another snow had blown in during the day, covering the sidewalks and their icy patches with deceptive white. Walking home, I hit one of those spots and landed on my butt. Stevie, hearing my loud exhale from a few steps ahead, returned to give me a hand. I brushed the snow off my backside and Stevie attempted to straighten the crushed Valentine box. When we reached the street where he turned, I watched the skinny figure under its bulky covering trudge up the incline. Lily wasn't the only puzzle in my world. It would take the progression of many years to untangle the Gordian knot that was my friend Stevie.

* * *

The next morning, my parents' conversation penetrated the gauzy veil of dreams that often preceded my waking. Daddy's rumble was indecipherable until Mom's voice posed a question: "Who was the child?"

At his answer, I stormed the brightly lit kitchen in PJs and bare feet: "What about Lily?"

Daddy had come from outside, snow clinging to his trouser cuffs and galoshes. Seated at the table, cigarette smoke drifting above her head, Mom gathered me onto her lap and wrapped my feet in the skirt of her chenille robe, an action I remembered from earlier days.

"I'll tell her, Raymond," she said. He followed his snowy footprints to the door as though relieved of a terrible duty.

I wasn't a child who cried easily, but I was one who expected the explanation adults got, not the watered down version handed out to kids. So Mom laid bare the pertinent, ugly facts: The school bus had stopped in front of Lily's house the evening before and she'd hopped off the step like any other day. As usual, when the driver engaged the clutch the bus drifted back before continuing up the grade. But this time, Lily had landed on an icy spot and slid behind the huge, crushing wheel. No one realized that she wasn't safely on the path until it was too late.

Later that morning, Mom walked me to school, something she hadn't done in a long time. Other mothers were there too and left their kids with a pat or a squeeze before returning to snowy sidewalks or cars idling at the curb. Miss Brothers announced that the next day our class would visit the funeral home in Zanesville, a few miles up the Muskingum River.

* * *

A subdued group of fifth-graders exited the school bus and ascended broad, snow-free steps. In the grand foyer a huge chandelier with uncountable bulbs cast a majestic glow. A grimly polite funeral director led us into a room where a casket sat on a bier. From where I stood, I could see only the edges of a silky pink lining, making it easier to imagine Lily back in the classroom, apart and isolated, but alive. The first group paused at the casket; some stared as they might at a rare specimen while others afforded Lily barely a glance. When it was my group's turn, my feet seemed to forget how to move, and it took a push from behind to propel me forward.

Mom had told me Lily would look like she was asleep, but that was not true. Lips frozen into a smile, hands clasped around a white rose, this Lily was more like the celluloid doll in my grandmother's dresser drawer than a real girl. Only the eyelashes were authentic, recalling the bright blue eyes they had shielded that first January morning as she stared out the window and their sweep against pale cheeks as she and Miss Brothers worked on the mailbox. Lily's hair, freed of its pigtails, lay loose and streaked with gold in the light of a headlamp.

Lily's parents stood in a shadowy corner, and Miss Brothers went over to speak to them. The mother exposed her agony for only a second before dropping her head and continuing to twist a damp handkerchief. The father's jarring voice and outsized motions as he reached for Miss Brothers' hand could well have been Uncle Hank's. I recognized the leering smile and felt my teacher's hesitation to have her hand swallowed in his. He must have felt it too because his face took on the injured expression I'd seen in Uncle Hank's when I recoiled from his advance. As though to shame me he would ask, "Don't you like your Uncle Hank, Missy?"

Lily's mother backed up to the wall as if for support and began to slide toward the floor. Her husband spoke harshly. "Shake it off, Ellen. This is no place to go to pieces."

Miss Brothers stepped in to support her while the funeral director opened a folding chair.

"Don't fuss over her," Lily's father told them. "It just makes her worse."

The look on Miss Brothers' face would have silenced a classroom, but the man didn't notice. His hungry, searching eyes scanned the room as though gauging reactions to the family drama and paused to study the prettiest girls. I willed those girls invisible, just as I did myself when Uncle Hank's eyes toured my body.

* * *

Back on the school bus, I scooted far over in my seat and rested my forehead on the cool, soothing glass. Kids shuffled into their seats and goofed off almost like normal. Having visited death that afternoon, they were ready to return to the safe and familiar. As for me, I'd lost trust in the familiar landscape of my world, and I wondered if I'd ever feel safe again.

Outside my window, a rash of flurries found their way to the ground, adding another dimension to the stained and trampled layers that had preceded them. At this rate, they would cover the ice that had sent Lily to her death in no time at all. I thought of snowfall's persistence to hide the ugliness of this world beneath a field of white. So much damage could be done under the guise of innocence.

Just before the bus pulled out, Stevie slid into the seat beside me, gray eyes heavy with thought, and we settled back for the ride home.

Sarah Smith

Small Talk

He fixin' roofs, she shrugs unapologetically
Half the roofs in this county sittin' in the kitchens
Better than workin' in that coal mine
That's the hardest work there is

Matter of fact, she says
Between draws on her cigarette
Smoke fills the hot, stale air between us
Her cheeks hollow out and I see

Lines that circle her mouth
Just like the ones in the trees
Sugar maple, beech, hemlock, oak
One line for each year

We sit on the splintered porch
Staring into the yard, I see a barn cat
Pick up her kittens with her teeth
Moving them away.

Dana Wildsmith

Patience
–James Still, Writer, U.S. Army, WWII

He'd never talked to me before
that day at lunch. He said,
One year I waited by the door.
I'd wake, get out of bed,

get dressed, go out and sit and watch
the people passing by.
I noticed how they moved. I watched
their faces, studied eyes,

their mouths. I taught myself to walk
the way they walked, to raise
my hand hello, to nod, to talk
a bit about the day's

ongoing drought or gully washer.
Last light, I'd head inside
to eat, to read. Darkness ushered
in the dreams again, so, first light,

I'd start over After a year
or so, I finally passed right well.
He stopped there, tipped back his chair.
Nothing else to tell.

Long time coming home from war,
I asked? He nodded *yes,*
studied me a moment more,
picked up his plate and left.

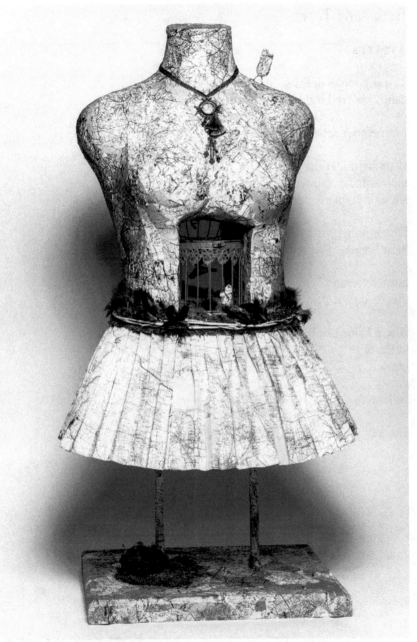

Alyson Annette Eshelman
Mapping Her Way

Beth Jane Toren

Tygrrrs

The sky looks nothing like it did then
candy colored lights outshine the galaxies

I remember saber tooth tygrrrs

sleeping under the stars
their soft fur and warm bodies
snuggling on all sides of me

Father mined
their bones

burned to run
this carousel

where I ride one's
hideous
plaster
glossy
caricature

The sky looks nothing like it did then

Lonormi Manuel

That Last Saturday in August

Ellen went missing on that last Saturday in August, a sticky-hot day alive with the threat of thunder and the drone of cicadas. She was sweaty and dusty by the time she coasted her scarred yellow Schwinn Flyer across the highway into the gravel forecourt of McClain's store. She leaned the bike against the corner of the building, not bothering with the kickstand, and went into the shadowy coolness to get a dozen eggs. Someone her parents knew had died, and her mother needed to make a cake, or maybe deviled eggs, or maybe both.

Ellen wasn't allowed to go past McClain's store. It squatted by the highway, catty-corner from the intersection where the dirt road began its snakelike crawl up the ridge. She was always careful about looking both ways. *People drive like maniacs on that road,* her father said, and she had made the trip to McClain's often enough to know he spoke the truth. Once, as she waited on the shoulder for traffic to pass, she had almost been hit by a young man in a foreign car who was fiddling with the radio and not minding the road. The front tire dipped onto the gravel shoulder, pulling the car with it. Just in time the driver saw her, screamed a word she couldn't hear, and jerked the car back onto the blacktop.

Two old fans hung from the tongue-and-groove ceiling and moved the air in the shadows, just enough to push the stagnant heat from corner to corner. Ellen stood beneath one of them, until the manufactured breeze dried her sweat-damp skin. She pulled a dozen eggs from a cooler that smelled like oil and shuddered with the effort of its motor, remembering to open the carton and check for cracked or broken eggs. She tucked the eggs under her arm and reached into the chill darkness of a chest-type cooler, her fingers searching the dark for an Orange Crush.

Mr. McClain's unmarried daughter put down her cigarette when Ellen set the eggs and the pop on the counter. Miss McClain punched the keys of an old-fashioned register, noted the total, and jotted the amount on a receipt pad that had Ellen's father's name printed in cramped letters across the top binding.

"Tell your mama I said hey," Miss McClain said.

"I will."

An iron bottle opener with the Coca-Cola logo hung on the wall by the door. Ellen wedged the dewy bottle beneath the opener and popped the cap, dropping it into her pocket. The screen door screamed as she went back into the heat and sunshine. The bench by the door was empty; she sat in the middle of it and drank the Orange Crush. She went back inside just long enough to exchange the empty bottle for her five-cent deposit, and gave the bottle cap to Miss McClain to give to her nephew who collected bottle caps.

And then she mounted her bike and headed home.

I always watch her cross the road, Miss McClain told the police later that evening. *She looked both ways, more than once, and then she stood on the pedals and crossed the blacktop and rode uphill as far as her legs would take her. I know she had to get off and walk part of the way, where it gets steep, but once she was under the trees I couldn't see her anymore.*

She knew not to stop for a stranger. Her parents reminded her, each time she left the house: *don't stop for strangers, don't speak to strangers, stay away from strange cars.* It was a good rule, one she always obeyed. But the narrow dirt road that snaked down the hollow to the two-lane blacktop highway seldom saw a stranger. The ridge road was outside the limits of county maintenance; you had to live there to know how to navigate the ruts and rocks between the ditches. Other people traveled the road—the mailman, the UPS truck, the blue bullet-shaped tanker that refilled the liquid propane tanks that hunkered by the houses—but those people weren't really strangers.

It took two days for the men and their dogs to find Ellen's body, hidden under broad leaves of sumac and bowed heads of elderberry at the bottom of the hollow, where a thin freshet trickled over moss-slick rocks. She lay on her back, eyes closed, hands crossed on her chest. Her hair, released from its ponytail, fanned out beneath her like cornsilks. Her pink t-shirt and cut-off jean shorts were dirty but undisturbed, and a smear of oil from the bicycle chain soiled one sock. One shoe had lodged in the brambles of the hillside; the other leaned against the bank of the stream, wet from toe to tongue. Orange Crush stained her lips, but no visible wounds or bruises marred her body.

It looked like, the sheriff told her parents, *she had just laid herself down to take a little nap, there at the bottom of the holler.*

The egg carton, half-open, spilled broken shells into a dark patch of ground a few yards away, surrounded by the tracks of possums and raccoons.

Ellen's yellow Schwinn Flyer was never found.

Jeanne Shannon

Along the Clinch River at Dungannon, Virginia

Low fields
dream in the haze

milkweed, mullein
ripen in corners of dusk

an aluminum moon
rising

Jeanne Shannon

When Panthers Roamed in the Blue Ridge

They lived in an old house

with long porches   miles from town   A dirt road full of ruts

Woods thick with white oak and maple and hornbeam
　　and rhododendron pink in the spring

They bought a phonograph   the Carter Family
and a radio   Lowell Thomas   news of the War

She got up every morning   long before daylight
built a fire in the cook stove

made hot cocoa   oatmeal   biscuit bread

then walked two miles
to ring the school bell at Osborne's Gap

the moon still up
　　　and a few stars

Sometimes she'd hear a panther   its chilling cry
only a shadow away

"I heard a wildcat in the woods this morning,"
she'd say.

The morning the Big Snow came
my father rode horseback to bring her home

Busy with drills on long division
　　　she hadn't noticed   the snow already
　　　three feet deep

Evenings around the firelight   She tatted
crocheted   embroidered   made patchwork morning glories

and perfect 5-pointed   cut-paper stars

Summers they planted   broomcorn   bleeding-hearts
carrots and beets   Kentucky Wonder pole beans

In the Fall of the Year   Mason jars
glowed on the cellar shelves

    tomatoes red as sunrise   bread-and-butter pickles
       Concord grapes in their lake of juice

Their second house   spider-legs bloomed in the yard
horseapple trees along the creek bank

She cried   when the coal was strip-mined

Later, on her wall a plaque that read

       In recognition of 35 years
       of faithful service
       to the education of the children
       of the Commonwealth of Virginia. . .

       Maple Grove, Trace Fork, Bear Pen, Osborne's
       Gap, Camp Creek, Sullivan Branch

Past ninety then   alone in her room at the nursing home
she told me things

       "When you were born   there was snow on the ground
       The doctor's car got stuck   down at Pardee
       but he got there in time

       It was just before daylight   the roosters
       had started to crow

       I knew you would be a girl

       I saw things I wanted to tell you
          but I never did."

Jeanne Shannon

Tulip Tree Standing in the North Fork of the Powell River, Appalachia, Virginia

> *Sometimes a tree tells you more than can be read in books.*
> *– C. G. Jung*

> *Tulip tree: A tall, deciduous, eastern North American tree,*
> Liriodendron tulipifera, *of the Magnolia family, having large tulip-like*
> *green and orange flowers, aromatic twigs, and yellowish, easily worked wood.*

Stalwart amid broken rocks in the center of the river, the restless and unforgiving river, carrying its dank cargoes of mud and human trash.

Stunted and small, assaulted endlessly by winds and stinging weathers. At the mercy of a waterfall that shows no mercy.

Sometimes a log washes against it, bending it double, but when the log is gone it straightens and stands up again.

It cannot grow into its tall cone shape. It cannot open its orange goblet-flowers, nor welcome birds to nest among its branches. How lonely it seems, how mute and solitary, under the glow of western sunsets, season after season.

When its sister trees along the riverbank break out in fragrant tulip blooms, what does it whisper on the wind?

(With thanks to Howard E. Cummins for his article "A Tree Grows in Appalachia" in the Big Stone Gap, Virginia Post.*)*

Roberta Schulz

The Two in One Junior (Song)

Oh, wash my soul   (Oh, wash my soul)
On the Two in One Junior.
Glide my sins   (Glide my sins)
over rippled glass.
Don't snag my heart   (Don't snag my heart)
in the Devil's laundromat.
Don't wring me out,   (Don't wring me out)
make a delicate pass.

I'm a hard luck stranger on a crooked road,
and I long to return to my home
But the mountains loom steep before that dear land of sleep,
and I fear that forever I will roam.

All the other travelers on this mountain path
wear the permapress coating of their kin.
But my cloth is threadbare, unraveling into air,
fraying weave held together by sin.

All the patchwork in the lost and found pray for a gentle hand
to dip them deeply in that water sweet that flows from a promised land.

I will thank you kindly if you use that board
dear Mama chose to keep our nighties clean
for there's no mercy in a tumble dry,
no forgiveness in a washing machine.

Welcome home. Oh, you are welcome here.
Feel at peace. Never fear.

A storyteller stands up on a stage
to share beginnings of this sacred place
how fog descended from the heavens before
true worth could be revealed.

Roberta Schulz

Like Horses (Song)

My mother always told me
If wishes were horses, beggars would ride.
I watched her make her wishes,
but then she'd toss each one aside

for laundry on weekends, for groceries,
and the daily office grind.
She'd smile at those salesmen,
pack up her blues and leave her wishes behind.

At times, when I was younger,
she'd sketch my portrait underneath a tree.
Then, tell of Aunt Loretta.
Her cautionary tale was meant just for me:

Don't wear those pierced earrings.
They'll stretch your ear lobes,
and they'll ruin your chance.
You'll end up a loose woman—
another victim of that mating dance.

One day my father left her
for a younger woman with pierced ears.
Mom bought herself some diamonds,
tiny studs to eradicate all her fears.

Poked through with those changes,
illuminated by refracted light,
she rides her own wishes like horses,
like horses, like horses

through the night.

Connie Kinsey

High-Tech Hillbilly Woman

I am a high-tech hillbilly woman.

I am wired, wireless and bluetoothed. I have a desktop computer, a tablet, a smart phone, a traveling computer, and then there is The Laptop. I would jump into a dumpster to save the laptop. On it I have photos, legal documents, all of my writing, and my passwords to the world. I have music files and video files. I have love letters and formal complaints. I have haiku. And recipes.

My life preserved in pixels. In bits and bytes, zeroes and ones.

I bought this model for the sound system. I listen to a lot of music on that thing. Sometimes, music is important to me. Other times I need silence, but when I want music, I want it good and loud. I load up a playlist and dance in front of the laptop, speakers blaring, body whirling.

The laptop is 17 inches and silver. The large screen lets me have more tabs open. I multi-task when on the laptop. Social media, writing, solitaire, email, and work. Garden plans and budgets. Photo editing and messaging.

My whole life is in there. Truly. I don't watch TV; I Facebook. I don't write letters; I have long rambling emails with family and friends. I have thousands of photos. Thousands just from two weeks in Spain alone. I have email going back to the early 90s. Yes, really. It's the archive of my life.

The laptop used to be slick and shiny but is now covered in crumbs and fingerprints. It's made of metal and silicon and wires and magic. I'm an IT person and I don't understand how it works. I blog from the laptop. I meet new people on the laptop. I reconnected with an old high school friend who is now my boyfriend while on the laptop. He and I communicate daily via the laptop. It's not a machine—it's a conduit.

I'd like it even better if it were blue. Blue is my favorite color, and the laptop is one of my favorite things. It's the first thing I check in the morning after pouring coffee and feeding the dogs; and it's the last thing I do at night.

It is incomparable, really.

The laptop picks up my memories and my moods, memes and statuses. I can sit in my comfortable chair and enter other worlds. I eat at the laptop. The flotsam and jetsam of my life end up there. I just brush it off. The machine needs a thorough cleaning as do most things in my life.

The keyboard is quiet. There is some noise—I can hear the keys click but it's not obtrusive. It's comforting. The sound of productivity. The sound of creativity. The sound of me being me.

I feel blessed to be living in this time. The cyber-revolution will be studied for years to come. I was on the internet before sound and pictures. Before music and photos. Before internet shopping. Before Wi-Fi and video. Back on a green screen with a flashing cursor. I hung out in Usenet—not the first, but one of the very first social internet gathering spots. Back when everybody on the 'net knew everyone else or at least recognized their email address. Those were great, heady times. We knew it was a revolution. We knew we were exploring frontiers. 1980s—I talked about my friends on the 'net. My son thought I was talking about a woman named Thanette. He drew a picture of her.

I hope that my grandchildren find my digital life interesting. I think by the time I have grandchildren, this will all be so old hat that the magic will be gone. It will be just a utility, like the phone, but now? Now, it's special. We are still on the frontier though it is less wild. Or maybe more. I think that depends on your perspective.

The laptop is awe, magic, and opportunity. It is my confidante and my muse. It houses my friends, my family, and my creativity. It is the medium I work in. It is my art.

I am a high-tech hillbilly woman.

Catherine Pritchard Childress

Blossoming Indigo

I coveted the Wranglers my brother wore
when we played outside—durable denim
seat impervious to rocks, sticks, glass shards
unearthed when we scooted toward the stream,
worn knees grass-dyed lucent chartreuse,
pockets deep enough to hold his morning finds—
bumboozers, bottlecaps, buckeyes—treasure
I had to secure in the dirty hem of my skirt—
what "ladies" wore to church, to play, to school
where other girls arrived each September
in Lees with pleats and pink pinstripes.
But they're pink! My rebuttal when my father
defended his edict with Deuteronomy 22:5,
declared jeans are for boys, refused
even my plea to try on one pair, *just to see—*
to take on each lean leg like I'd watched
my friends do; ease them over calves, knees,
shimmy past thighs, hips, around my waist,
look over my shoulder, discover curves
blossoming indigo—a woman in the glass
reflecting why he always said no.

Catherine Pritchard Childress

Portrait

I bathed and lotioned you to a pink sheen,
sponged away milk curdled in your folds,
dressed you in starched linen and leather
lace-ups—shoes mailed, with coupons clipped
from a Gerber cereal box—to be bronzed
so they could flank the photo your father
waited in the side-yard to capture.

He chose the cushioned rocker to prop you in,
dragged it out beside the fading Shrub Rose—
its blooms so much like my nipples, cracked
as your smacking lips drained my breasts
in twenty-minute intervals. Lullabies, rocking,
each day's routine subject to your rhythm.

He snapped three shots to wind the film.
I posed you in the chair's corner—certain
cherry arms and spindles could not keep you
from toppling heavy-headfirst into overgrown grass—
backed away from his composition, away from you.

Your constant hunger hanging heavy—
his, looming over a four-poster bed.
Your soured spit-up on my shoulder—
his musk between my thighs. Your weight
stretched like every month's last paycheck
across my hips—his, thrust against them.

I didn't tell you I needed my body back
from you—from him; didn't tell you
lullabies are lies (pictures too),
that diamond rings turn brass, glass
breaks, babies fall, bronzed shoes tarnish,
and mothers disappear

                              just outside the frame.

Kari Gunter-Seymour
Cicada Shell Can't Sing No Blues

Tonja Matney Reynolds

Shoes

The sitter was sick, but Jen had a deadline at work. She thought she'd be able to finish it at home during the baby's nap, but he was teething and fussy and never went down. Her daughter Katie could have played with him until their dad showed up to take them for the weekend, but another first grade cupcake party had her wired. Two birthdays on one day. Double chocolate Friday.

Katie crawled this way and that on the back of the sofa and peered out the living room window like a nervous cat at the zoo. Her shoes still on, Mary Janes. No wonder the couch was so dirty now and worn. Jen and her now-ex had spent hours choosing the fabric for it, their first purchase when they bought this house that was supposed to be their forever home.

Jen pulled the shoes off Katie's feet and tossed them onto the pile of shoes by the front door. All the while, the baby gnawed and sucked on his hand.

An email from her boss made Jen's heart race now. How much longer would she be? With the baby squirming in her arms and running his drooly hands through her hair, she typed her response. *Day's end.* A slight misdirection. He'd think she meant six, but it was looking like midnight.

When the baby started fussing more, Jen started pacing. Patting his back. Telling him it would be okay, which calmed him a little and calmed her none.

She sat on the floor with the baby on her lap and sorted the shoes. A tiny pair of Velcro gym shoes that never stayed on the baby's feet. Katie's red glitter flats like the ones Dorothy wore. House slippers. Pink galoshes. Jen's black Mary Janes beneath Katie's girl-sized pair, identical except for the size. Not a womanly shoe, but practical. Comfortable. Not the slightest bit sexy, but who had time for sexy?

***

When the doorbell finally rang, the baby was inconsolable.

Katie grabbed the Dorothy shoes and then her Mary Janes and finally settled on the galoshes despite the lack of rain. She ran outside, leaving a messy pile of shoes behind, and hugged her dad while Jen searched for the tiny Velcro pair.

A woman stood next to him on Jen's porch that had been *their* porch. A woman in a too-tight, too-short skirt. Wearing sexy, strappy shoes with pointed heels.

Jen tried to hand him their still-unshoed, crying baby. "Have them home Sunday morning."

He took a step back, arms at his sides. "We're just going to a movie. I'll have Katie home before dark."

She stared at him and he stared back while Katie skipped to the car with the stiletto-heeled stranger.

"I need to work," Jen said.

"I can't take a baby to a movie."

"You don't need a movie. You need to take your kids. You promised you'd take Katie to the zoo. To see the cats."

"I thought *you'd* want to take them."

There it was. Every despicable thing he'd done in their marriage, including leaving her with an infant, was done for *her*. To help *her*.

She thrust the baby toward him, but her ex's arms were limp. He wouldn't even take the tiny shoes. After a five second standoff, he turned from her and walked down the porch steps.

Something inside of her snapped like a too-tight rubber band. She winged a baby shoe at his head. And then another. The baby giggled.

He rushed back to her, up the stairs. Battle on.

With the baby on her hip, Jen ran inside and reloaded. Through the open door, she whizzed shoes at him. Baby shoes. Dorothy flats. House slippers. The big and small Mary Janes. One after the next until her lawn that had been *their* lawn was littered with shoes.

When the battle ended, her ex marched to his car and opened the back door. Katie got out. As he drove away, Katie gathered the Mary Janes and brought them to her mom. Together, they collected the rest of the shoes one at a time, looking up to see if the car would return. Each biting her lip, blinking back tears. As if something or someone coming down the road could change everything all in an instant.

The baby started crying again.

Karen Nelson Whittington

Love and Obey
~ *in memory of my grandmother*

With God
and all her kinfolk
squeezed into the shabby chapel,
she promised to love and obey;
she was here to stay.
Day, after day,
after year, after year
went by
and she thought she'd leave, but
the babies needed their daddy
and every year brought
another, and another
mouth to feed
and bill after bill to pay,
so you couldn't
just up and walk away.
And away
went the children, grown,
grown—
with lives of their own,
until nothing stood in her way
but the man, sitting silently
in the quiet, forgotten space,
asking without words, asking
so softly that she strained to
hear him above the hum of
memories gallivanting within
the rooms of the outgrown house,
asking her to stay, please stay,
until it was he, he who slipped away.
And so, content, here she'll stay,
until with God, she'll fly away…
She'll take her leave, her hat and key,
lock the door and fly; she'll fly
away.

Barbara Marie Minney

Blackwater River Canyon

Everything was in black and white then
   except the keepsakes
living on in my consciousness
   like fragile eight-millimeter film
moving through a hot and noisy projector
   breaking at the most inopportune moment.

Isolated in my developing understanding
   sitting on an immense boulder
down in the yawning canyon
   surrounded by stately pines
and towering oaks
   leaves turning bloody in the crispness of autumn.

Hypnotized by the changing hues
   and the fury of the white water
erupting over the worn rocks
   crying into the amber stream
colored by the crayons of spruce and hemlock trees
   I'm overwhelmed by an unfamiliar sense of sanctuary.

 A turkey buzzard
   ripples across the tides in the dusky sky
percolating across the Allegheny Mountains
   the smell of woodland muskiness
titillating my nose
   with the perfume of darkness.

A lone cardinal hollers for its mate
   and maybe for me too
shapes constantly changing
   as the pulsating water washes over jagged rocks
poking their heads out
   like drunken sailors moving with the ripples.

Stretching a quivering hand
   into the frosty water
and taking out a spent .22 shell
   brass luminous in the paling light

I bring it to my mouth
    savoring the restorative water.

Imperceptible droplets of moisture
    climb onto the breeze
washing against my face
    like tears of absolution
momentarily getting outside of myself
    to experience freedom.

Mary Lucille DeBerry

Barn Hill

A smooth, easy but exhilarating climb.
Meadow hilltop. Flat for flying homemade kites.

The barn long gone. A nighttime fire.
Flashing flames. Helpless neighbors racing.

A glare illuminated the town till the light
of day was surpassed, the Ritchie Gazette

editor recalled. On May 10, 1879, he was
aroused from slumber by the courthouse bell.

No foundation stones. Just a roofless grassy
dugout, reminiscent of an amphitheater.

The building was a mass of flames
shooting far up into the heavens.

Autumn olive encroaches on daffodil rows.
Hedgerow vultures stretch wake-up wings.

Former acreage subtracted by eminent domain
to ensure no structures near a potential lake.

Not a breeze strong enough to stir a leaf.
If so, half the town would have been in ruins.

Treasured woodland paths overgrown.
Boundary fences tangled, rusted orange.

Signs: "No Hunting."   "No Trespassing."

Note: The newspaper account is found in *Ritchie County Crimes & Calamities:*
Reports from the Local, State and National Press,1847-1922 compiled (2011) by
John M. Jackson

Stephanie Kendrick

What to Expect: Unplanned Pregnancy, Postpartum Anxiety and Too Many Dead Cats

I suppose a woman tripped into a man,
decided she liked the ways that her skin
folded against his skin, both hairy and cold.
I suppose she kept her skin touched to his,
smiled at the way his warmed
and softened on her own. And as it goes,
I suppose they made a baby.

The smell of falafel and spearmint lingered mid-air between the muffled noises of patrons and my partner's parents. They were all trying to talk over the sounds of a mizmar oozing through a black speaker in the corner of the restaurant that guided the clinks of chains draped over a belly dancer's hips. It is difficult to say which of the senses triggered the nausea first. I excused myself from the table and power-walked to the bathroom, barely making it, and stayed until I was sure I was empty. He and I hadn't even been together 2 years before I came down with "the flu." Days of vomiting and severe fatigue turned into weeks.

My professors stopped excusing absences and the university clinic said there was nothing more they could do. "The strain is just so bad this year," they would tell me. During the check-ins at my desperate visits, a young woman gripped a clipboard and read the same questions each time: "Do you use tobacco products? How many alcoholic drinks do you consume per week? Are you sexually active?" and so on.

I lied when answering most of her questions. I won't speak for all twenty-one-year-old women; however, at that time, those questions did not overlap with my concept of general health. I was skinnier than I had ever been and had a busy social life, which was all the validation needed to prove I was doing everything right. The last time I visited the clinic, I was starting to worry. Pregnancy had finally become a concern when the typical 10–14-day lifecycle of a flu came and went. I again fibbed my way through clipboard woman's questions, this time adding a detail to the question of sex. "I think I *did* miss a couple pills a few weeks ago." Still, no test was administered at the clinic.

When I saw the doctor, she handed me some anti-nausea medication and said, "Looks like you're having a really hard time fighting off that flu, huh?"

"Yeah, no shit," I thought.

As I sauntered back to the table through the thick smell of jasmine and curry wafting from the kitchen, I held my breath and prayed to the universe that I really was empty. I apologized to his parents for not eating. The next day, I bought a pregnancy test and confirmed that it was never "the flu."

> *I suppose their baby fit into the folds*
> *of skin already warmed and softened,*
> *kept safe with smiles and the practice*
> *of never looking away.*
> *I suppose it cooed and wooed them,*
> *hollowed their breaths until every whisper*
> *felt weightless, like nothing at all.*

At first it was always in an elevator. I didn't know what a lucid dream was until the week after we brought him home. Sleep was different, not something that was sought after, but something that happened upon me, like a Charley horse or hiccups. I was so exhausted that my body would shut down before my brain knew how to react. And I would be there with my son, in an elevator, always between two strange men. He'd go limp in my arms. My mouth opened and nothing would come out, not even breath. Try it. Open your mouth and scream without letting anything escape-no sound, no breath, nothing. I would try to call out until realizing I was sleeping. My head knew that it wasn't real, but I couldn't get myself out of that damn elevator. I couldn't throw him from my arms, couldn't wake myself. The only thing that could snap me back was his cry, which happened at least every two hours those first weeks. Babies are insatiable ... alive.

At seven months, my partner and I finally told the rest of our family—our parents already knew—that we were expecting. We had grappled with the choices that were available, but that is a different story for another time. I was ashamed. I had no prior experience of celebrating birth. Babies were barriers to the cycle I was supposed to break. Truth be told I was spiraling downward well before "the flu," but there I was—seven months pregnant, a college drop-out, unemployed, without the wherewithal to keep a cactus alive, let alone a human. So, I decided to adopt a cat.

In our town, feral cats roam the streets. It is a famous issue that is brought up regularly at various town council meetings and in scathing letters to the editor. Some folks make a regular habit of shooting or trapping the cats, and then there are the good Samaritans who humanely catch the street-wise mousers and pay the out-of-pocket expense to "fix" them and find good homes. It was a regular occurrence to get a call from a friend to see if our home could be one of those good ones. So when a pal reached out at a time I was feeling particularly needy, I readily accepted. There is something about kittens that converts even the coldest and virile of men to big softies, and I needed that energy. They refuse not to be adored. They pull smiles from you without asking, and their bellies make a sound that serves as constant affirmation that they love you back. Our friend dropped it off and we had her for one night before our dog laid on it while we were sleeping. When I found it that morning, lifeless and covered in dog slobber, I was gutted, but not yet convinced that I was being targeted by the universe. No, it wasn't until the week after that I became absolutely sure I was being existentially punished for the shame and doubt I felt about becoming a mother, and all the bad decisions I had made up to that point. The week after the dog suffocated the cat with too much love (this is how I imagine it happened. I was asleep and don't know this for sure) I was having a cigarette on my front porch (because remember, I was doing absolutely fine and needed to make no changes to my health whatsoever) and heard a high-pitched mewing coming from under the porch. An abandoned kitten, barely able to raise its little head, laid emaciated and covered in crust. I snatched it up with hopes of redeeming my most recent failure. The crust was easy to bathe away, but the poor creature had given up already. I stayed up all night trying to get water and milk in it. I tried a bottle purchased for the baby who was nearing his move-out date, tried my fingertips and palms but at about 4 in the morning, it took its final breath in my lap, emptied itself of any fluids left inside. Another reminder that I would absolutely fail at being a mother.

> I suppose the woman loved the baby,
> and felt sure that it loved her, every cry
> a reminder of its need for her.
> I suppose that fear only lingers as long
> as it is needed, dissipates with time,
> reappears when uncertainty emerges.
> I suppose motherhood is always uncertain.

We didn't provide a home to another creature until he left my body. In the morning of his second day outside of me, while his father slept like a baby in my stiff, narrow hospital cot, I held him in my arms and stared at him while he slept. I was relieved at the ease with which he nestled so comfortably in my arms, and at the competence I showed by stabilizing his sweet head in my palm. I lifted him to my face and slowly smelled his hair, whisps of gold, barely there. He smelled like me, in that, he didn't smell at all. I think of the way a mother cat wastes no time licking the hell out of her kittens as soon as they return to her after having been held and loved by humans. I could do the research, but my maternal instincts (few as they are) tell me she is removing strange scent from them, rendering them hers again. He was perfect. The moment was fleeting, as all peaceful moments are, and he began stirring and wrinkling his nose for milk, or a diaper change, or because I was not comfortable … it's really hard to tell when you don't speak baby. In a panic, I moved to return him to his plastic, sterile bassinet with trembling hands so that I could determine my next move. I was alone in that room. No nurses. Partner fast asleep. "Why didn't I read the goddamn baby books?!" I thought. As I lowered him into the bassinet I slipped, dropping him a few inches rather than laying him gently. His perfect little head bounced on the plastic causing his perfect little face to contort and squirm for the longest second to ever pass before he screamed. I scooped him up and we cried together, and in the most beautiful case of serendipity that has not since been matched in my world, my mother walked into our hospital room and took us both into her arms.

I don't remember what she said to me in that moment, but I remember she made me laugh and let me know that it wouldn't be the last time that I screwed something up as a mom. She knew the pain and the ubiquity of this too well. A working-class, single mother of three, she perpetually had her hands full; and we weren't easy kids, but that's another story for another time. I learn best by making big mistakes, and let me tell you, I get that honest. I think she saved me that day, and I never told her that. Sometimes the only reason I write a piece is to leave behind bits of things I never can bring myself to say out loud.

The dread that came with motherhood never left me. A decade later, I still have nightmares of him dying in my arms. Every time I punish him, I ache with thoughts of what my harshness might lead him to do, and whenever he is not with me, thoughts of awful ends play out in my head on loop. The anxiety and panic remained undiagnosed for 8 years before I discovered that I had postpartum anxiety. I always understood those feelings as repercussions of my poor decisions, symptomatic of maternal ineptness and nods from the universe (whatever that means) that I didn't deserve a healthy baby. Before becoming educated on hormones, genetic components and the impacts of tremendous stress on my brain and body, I would say to myself, "this is what you get for missing your birth control, for dropping out of school, for the almost-adoption, for the cigarettes and the pot…" and it would continue ad nauseam. Thanks to a therapist who relied just as much on the power of sage and Brene Brown as she did on actual science, I am now about 98% confident that I am not being perpetually punished. I cannot emphasize enough the power that came from understanding my brain and body. My son thrives, and he doesn't know it, but he saves me too; not in the "I finally have purpose" sort of way—There is something installed in children that makes them a little too comfortable calling out dishonesty and contradiction in their parents, and if the parent knows what's good for them, they listen.

I suppose the woman learns to show love
to herself by listening to the baby,
who is not afraid
to open its mouth wide, scream into the air,
"feed me, clean me, hold me."

Lee Peterson

Election Day
—*November 2008*

Long loose days inside—we step off the porch,
out from the cocoon of new life.
Campaign signs dot the walkways and yards.

My daughter of six months sits strapped to my chest.
The dog lurches ahead and nearly tips us over.

A grey sky rests, flat cap on the day.
No snow. The hillside a dying flame.

Down in the heart of town the cathedral dome
looms. Thumb tip against the Alleghenies.

Visual mark on the landscape
calling/recalling what—the devout?

The mother whose name is spoken
only in light of the son's?

I was born in Obama, she'll say once she's able.
But now—not knowing—we step out of the bingo hall.
On two legs, on four—we step into the air.

Lee Peterson

Inheritance

My grandmother's eyes are failing her out among the saguaros. So far from here—our Alleghenies, our April snows. I describe you to her, say your eyes are blue still, at nine months—as many days in our world as you were in only mine. Born on the prairie, she tells me: *Westerners' eyes are blue, from looking up, from so much sky.* The heavens so near and below them land—acres and miles. The vast expanse. Mountains' white caps. Fence posts mark the earth like dark fingers rising up. Back East in Pennsylvania we sit by the picture window. You look out—intent. Bouncing on my lap, a spring ready to pop. So eager for the blue, for birds on branches and wires, for snows. Inside our brick walls you've begun to climb—stairs, tables—all traversed. Not having learned to return things to their place, you unbuild. Studious in your destruction. Certain only of the need to tear down. You are becoming human. Child of the West, of the East and South. In your eyes—skyscrapers and sky. Wilson, Katz, and Cashion. From pavement, from Ivy walls. From prairies and taxi cabs. From piedmont and mill towns long gone. From oceans. Child of the middle. You've come to tear it down. Tear it down. Tear it down.

Susan Truxell Sauter

On the Nation's News
Inspired by Natalie Diaz's "It Was The Animals"

I could take the advertisements,
the vitamins needed, cleaning
products, the lizard-logo insurance.
I could not take the stiff answer-men,
the same hulls featured at 5, 6, 7 pm
News ad infinitum, him-hymn.
I could take the rigid window frame
even the immovable mahogany desk.

I could not take the window's glass
that mirror the men, men
who've always been in charge.
I could not take their smothering dark suits,
the difference-defying fabric that covers
skin color, age spots, support hose, prostheses.

I could not take the metal flag-pole,
slippery and polished, dark patina of history erased.
I could not take the imagined future red stain
—starry globules of female tissue, marring
the pole's hanging cloth—its white lines
blood-clotted at blue's edge.
I could not take the deflated celebratory balloon
skittering across the nation's lawn
hollow as a woman's ruptured uterus,
the husk collected into a scented trash bag.

For a moment, the glittering lies broke.
I watched products sanitize porcelain.
I could take the cleanest toilet, yes,
its glistening porcelain.

Elizabeth Tussey

My Mother's Offering to the River Ohio:

This city loses land, limps back to
the silt-soot, swelling with barge scars.

She rises from new shores, mucked with river
and grief, bearing strange gifts: pen cap, flip-flop.

chatters of long drags through hospital hallways
heart ensnared by box-springs at river bottom.

She brings jars of buttons, mined from the duplex: detritus
of her loneliness. They layer over dormant mayflies.

When they cross break-walls again he will be dust. Come
August and his wraith recedes with the waters and leaves only

the haunt of feature across my face. A salt stain
of heavy brows, a tendency towards leaving too soon.

Annette Kalandros

I Am More

I am more than breath or bones.
I am the Melungeon veins
of my many great-grandmothers
as they run through the coal mines
of West Virginia into Kentucky and Tennessee.

I am more than breath or bones.
I am my mother's and grandmother's blood
flooding the snow melt rivers
of Appalachia.

I am more than breath or bones.
I am my mother's iron ore,
her steel torn from the hollows
among the mountains of West Virginia
in the time of the Great Depression.

I am more than breath and bone,
I am the centrifuge
of history and heritage
of spirits and earth
of women who held
up mountains
for their children.

I am more than breath and bone.
We, my foremothers and I,
mother the culmination
of the next generations
to hold up the sky,
the sun, the stars, the moon
for their children.

Diana Ferguson
Stop

Eve Odom

Animal Instincts

One morning, I took my dog Luna for a walk. She is a skittish black and white, short hair border collie. Super smart but terribly scared of her own shadow. We were on our normal route to a wide side yard next to the apartment where we were living. It was cold and a hard frost covered the ground that sparkled iridescent with the morning light. The frozen grass softly crunched under each step. A black chain link fence separated the yard from a large wooded natural habitat that had a nice stream running through the property. Most of the trees were bare having let go of their leaves in the last few weeks, and you could see through the once heavily concealed area. As Luna and I first entered the yard, I spotted a large doe across the fence. She immediately saw me too and froze. The doe and I looked at each other for a while and then I said, "Hi pretty girl, you just takin' a morning walk too?" Luna never saw her, too busy smelling the dog urine of those before us, so after a few moments we released one another from our locked gaze and moved on.

A few feet later, I spotted a large white mass in the trees. This stopped me in my tracks. It sat perched on a lower tree limb. It had to be a white owl, from its sheer size and color. I was stunned. This was very special; I could feel it. I waited for a minute, watching for movement but I didn't see the slightest twig stir. Slowly, without making a noise, I pulled out my phone and tried to zoom in on it but couldn't really get close enough for the ultra-closeup shot. After snapping a few pictures, I slid the phone back into my pocket. I was certain it was an owl, but I wasn't going to jump the fence onto private property to get a closer look, not to mention Luna would go ballistic if she saw it. So, after hovering for far too long, we continued on our walk. When I returned to the apartment, I excitedly explained to my husband, Mitch, my discovery.

"I saw a white owl!" I said, unwrapping from my layers of clothes.

"What?" he said. I pushed the photos in front of him. He took the phone and swiped through, looking at each one intently.

"Oh, cool," he said studying them.

Later that day, Mitch and I were driving down I-26 and I saw another white bird. "Oh my God, there's another white bird!" I screamed in delight pointing out the window. I got a better look at this one. It had a round, white belly and a red streak on its head, which Google identified as a Red Headed Woodpecker. "That's the second white bird I've seen today," I declared with amazement and self-amusement. This all must mean something, I thought. I tried to raise all my earth baby energy and tap into the vibration of the natural world around me and bring my intuition into focus. What were all these animals trying to say to me? I tried to empty my mind and let it come to me. I imagined rivers of energy just pouring into me. The thought that came back around was: *you are going to have a visitor coming soon.* That was all I could think. And that very night, I did. I got my very first hemorrhoid.

We had just bought a new house and were in the process of painting it before we moved in. We spent all day walking the aisles of Lowes and shopping for materials. We loaded our cart with rollers, drop clothes, sanding squares, edging tools, rags, basically the entire paint section. That night we sanded, edged, and rolled. And then we sanded, edged, and rolled again. Tin Smith by Sherman Williams was a color I could live with. Was it blue or was it gray?

Before we headed back to the apartment, we unloaded boxes full of things we probably should have thrown away. Lamps, bike parts, and other typical moving items that you always wonder how you accumulated. There was one box that I tried to pick up, but strain as I must, I could not pick it up. It must have been full of bricks, which isn't surprising because Mitch never throws anything away. And I think, at that very moment, a small, hard, and very irritating little monster lump appeared near my anus. On our ride back to the apartment, I scooted my bottom across the truck seat as we drove down the interstate, trying to soothe this newfound irritation. After turning on the seat warmers, I wiggled around trying to eliminate whatever problem was taking over back there, wondering why my ass was suddenly itching like I had wiped myself with poison ivy. Oblivious to my dilemma, Mitch silently drove us back. When I finally got to a bathroom, I was mortified when my young, un-sun spotted hand grazed over a lump that should only be found in the elderly. I immediately got my phone out so I could see what was going on back there, but my instincts already knew, this earth baby knew. A Hemorrhoid. An external hemorrhoid to be exact. It was confirmed via photo on the screen in front me. I was falling apart.

In the car on the way to grab some food, Mitch complained about how he thought he had COVID. I said, "You wanna hear my new illness?"

"You have COVID too?" he said. The sunlight pushed through the windows, giving the impression of warmth on that cold morning.

"No, worse."

"Worse than COVID?" He looked at me like I was crazy.

"I have a hemorrhoid."

White rushed over his face. Before that exact moment, I have never seen my husband not want to have sex with me so much.

"Oh my God. What? How?" He said, disgust draping every word that rolled off his tongue.

A small laugh escaped my lips because he was so floored by this declaration, that was somehow even worse than his theoretical COVID diagnosis. But of course, this was his tenth COVID self-diagnosis.

"I think tryin' to pick up that box last night."

That week he would randomly ask me if I was still sick. "Sick?" I would say confused by his question.

"You know," whispering, "the hemorrhoid."

"Oh yeah, I still have that," I would say seriously, but laughing a bit to myself. Didn't this man see me give birth to our son?

I spent much of the week taking baths, relaxing, and sitting with a heating pad pushed up between my butt cheeks. All in all, it turned out not to be so bad for me. Also, I insisted that I couldn't lift anything else during our move. "Sorry, that might hurt the ole' hemorrhoid!" I sang almost blissfully and waddled away. Where others might have been embarrassed by their little friend, I leaned into it. When I went grocery shopping and they asked if I needed help out to my car, I said, "Yes, I believe I do because I got a terrible hemorrhoid." Or when we went to a restaurant and they were seating us at a table, "Oh, we're going to need a booth. I'm in a delicate position," leaning in, "Hemorrhoid," I whispered. People were usually so shocked that they were always willing to help.

After a few weeks, it had shrunk back down to a very tiny spot, and the throbbing itching had subsided. My visitor, whose relationship started out very irritating but progressed into something very special, peaking on friendly, had almost left me as suddenly as it appeared.

Our moving process was slow, especially since I stopped lifting boxes. A week later, I took Luna for another walk in the side yard at the apartment. I was so excited, hoping to see more wildlife now that I was in tune with my energy, chakras aligned, and obviously vibrating with the highest of frequencies. Certainly, my aura was shining freaking amazing hues of blue. I searched the woods eagerly. I looked for any sign of movement. Then I saw it. The white owl in the same spot I had seen it a week ago in broad daylight. I knew right then it wasn't an owl. Seeing a white owl in daylight is almost impossible but seeing it twice in the same spot in broad daylight, well that is not an owl. It was white trash perched on a low limb. So much for my animal instincts. I pulled out my green plastic poop bag, picked up my dog's steaming mound, threw it in the pet garbage can, and walked back to the apartment.

Anna Egan Smucker

Miss J

Spring, when the waters of Corbin and Glady forks
  swirl high, you might run aground where they meet,
  churning, whirling around Turtle Rock Island.

Years ago, an artist looked at its banks
  littered with rocks; imagined a home,
  a new life tuned to water and woods.

From up the hollow, she hired boys with muscles.
  Troublesome, she'd heard, but they knew stone,
and so with wheelbarrows and cement
  they began her house, a tall round tower, a slate roof.

After she bailed the boys out of jail *twice,* they built
  whatever she wanted, took to calling her "Miss J."
And now on that island where stone flanks gardens,
  beds a maze of paths, flags a patio, and anchors
    a house, a world, a life, she is old,

almost blind. Says she's not afraid of the new guys camping,
  rowdy up the creek. If they make trouble, she'll just call
her "bad boy" friends, now young grandfathers, but still known
    she says, for their shotguns *and* short tempers.

Mitzi Dorton

Mama's Ballerinas

Mama recalled being sent to a lady's house to pick up a winter coat,
How warm it felt wrapped around her, with the snow peppering down.
Didn't have sense enough to feel ashamed, she said,
Leapt and danced all through the holler,
past the coal camp houses!
*****
I think that's the reason Mama bought me a gold trashcan,
pretty fancy, a dancer with a pastel glazed net tutu on the front.
Rhinestones sprinkled in the background,
always a temptation for my friends to pick off,
which never bothered me, just Mama
She afforded me ballet lessons too,
But I had little interest in that
or the gold ballerina waste basket.
there most of my childhood,
… with missing rhinestones.

When my eighth birthday rolled around,
I wanted that cake I saw with my friend at the Giant supermarket,
a plastic doll in the middle,
the pastel icing frothed in layers of lilac, pink or emerald
as her dress.
Mama said the doll looked cheap and tacky,
Paid for a large sheet cake instead,
Topped with a porcelain ballerina wearing a crown,
and a buttery trio of roses.
****
My trashcan fell by the wayside
missing for fifty some odd years,
I still own the ballerina cake topper.
one knee bent in pose,
her neck broken and reglued
from where she rattled around in the drawer
in different moves.
I can't explain why I kept her
or reattached the head,
except that she was important to that little girl of the 1930s,
who danced home in a used coat.

Tina Parker

Learning from Home

While places like ours wear on the nation's nerves
We hit the hairpin curves.
We show our daughters strip-
Mined mountains, rail beds, boarded-
Up UMWA buildings.
We want them to learn from what we've lost.
Want the confederate flag
Curtains and car decals to take
On greater meaning.

Oh how they long to vote.
They want to leave,
Go anywhere big.
They've learned what it is to hate.

Look at the pretty birds they say
And wave middle fingers out the car windows.
Even in their dreams they cuss
And rail *No effing way.*

McKenna Revel

My Father's Father's Frog

It was all uphill,
Though no one could have told me that.

It was all uphill,
until it wasn't, but my breasts were,
and my body was too heavy to put the effort in
and my jeans were no longer stained with sidewalk chalk that I used
to color the gravel roads into rainbows.

It was all uphill,
those walks with my father's father,
through our muggy blood and his crops that raced toward one lone gate.

It was all uphill,
so it's lucky I grew up tall and with pointed tobacco stick teeth
and an affinity for my grandmother's herbs hidden
between potatoes and in the branches of cherry trees grown too high
above the faraway sea.

It was all uphill,
until it wasn't, and I wasn't,
and I was seven again with grandfather looking me dead in the face to
remind me that if I sprinted too far ahead of him I would lose
all humanity,
turn into some green, ugly, squatting thing,
a frog too busy
croaking.

Whitney Folsom
Divination

Susan O'Dell Underwood

Holler

I saw the best minds of my generation outsourced, exported from the
    Mountain South, lured by the shiny metropolis, seduced by suburban
    retail and big salaries and common ground with people who never
    heard of Appalachia, or who pronounce it wrong.
My cousins high-tailed it out of here—
    the epidemiologist in San Francisco, curator of master drawings in
    Rome, the librarian, corporate lawyer, NASA consultant, geneticist,
    marine biologist, the naval officer in Hawaii, my engineer brother
    designing war weaponry in Texas, all of them flying home for
    holidays, and funerals of relatives who never once stepped foot on a
    plane.
They count me lucky, to keep on living here, where the standards (they
    say to my face) are low, at least.
They say I'm an enviable two-hour drive from where our family land—
    still in the family—runs from hill to hill, in a holler cut through by
    the South Holston River.
They say they're jealous, of my meager house with English ivy and
    moss, my brief walk on cracked sidewalks to my college office,
    past defunct, run-down, boarded-up small town drear.
They say at least I'm geographically close to home.
Same as I do, they still call it *home*,
    but don't realize I'm not any closer to those roots than they are,
that I might as well be as far gone as any of them in exile,
that the leftover family land isn't deeded to me,
that the family that was ours is mostly dead and gone, anyway,
that the culture they idealize is past, as distant from me as it is from
    them, my head in a book instead of bumping a cow's udder; my life
    behind a desk instead of behind a plow; my yard full of shade trees
    and grass to mow,
    no front porch, no back porch, no room or sun to grow a garden,
    even if I knew how; my house with internet cables connecting me to
    students
    who ask in emails about the region's literature I've assigned:
    What's an outhouse? What's fat back? What's a pig in a poke?

In dark days I ask myself why it has to be me left to teach what's history
    now, why me, keeping the antique stories and old names of this part
    of the country, Appalachia, America, as if the language and terrain
    were barb-wired into me, when some days, I swear, I'd just as soon

put to some other use in some other place the future my ancestors
    pictured for me, hopeful I'd have a better, easier, more refined life than
    theirs, than this.
Even right here, I live in my time, though.
I need skills they'd never have dreamed, merging into interstate traffic,
    booking hotel rooms that cost what an acre of land used to, standing
    in line for a latte,
    taking subways and metros and buses when I get out in the *real
    world*.
I have done as much as I could to earn and enjoy my peoples' sacrifices
    before me.
I have obtained the highest degree in my field.
I have taken a train through the Alps and flown in a jet over Greenland,
    and I have stood in the Colosseum in Rome and seen the Mona Lisa
    in the Louvre.
I have hiked the Wonderland Trail at Mt. Rainier and stood in the cold
    Pacific.
I have ordered sushi in Kansas City while I listened to jazz I could
    understand fine,
    and I've eaten calamari right out of Monterey Bay with just the right
    wine.
And I know which fork to use for my salad.
I have driven through the Holland Tunnel and gone to Broadway plays,
    and I've eaten a slice in Brooklyn and a knish in Central Park.
I have read—and taught—the finest books ever written,
    and learned when I was young to play the piano.
I know Beethoven from Mozart,
I know suri alpaca from cashmere, fine bourbon from fine Scotch,
    polenta from spoon bread, mac and cheese from pasta quattro
    formaggi.
I have seen and smelled and tasted as far as I can get from where I was
    raised, so far I think I can't stand ever to go home again,
    and so far I panic I'll never get all the way back home again.

There are some days when I know I'm lucky I can't ever escape, that it's
    my duty, my call right here to teach kids who are the first in their
    families to go to college.
They read sonnets and write essays about sonnets, and soon they're
    tempted against their will to write sonnets, and stories, and papers on
    Faulkner and Foucault.
All the time, running in place—this place—they are leaving a little bit,
    never suspecting my ruse, my real agenda:
that someday their parents and cousins and grandparents will say good-
    bye to them because I have helped prove
that they are smart and strong enough to leave our beautiful, heart-

breaking hills,
that they've been born and raised to get the hell out, nothing for them
    here,
no cyber-commute far enough,
no library big enough to contain them,
no museum that's going to quench their desire for color, color, color,
no cocktail party too sophisticated, not to mention noise and lights and
    big paychecks and every rich taste at their hungry fingertips.
Like them, I have been starved every day of my life,
thinking I should just sell my birthright, get out while I still can,
thinking sometimes I've been a rube, cheated, left behind in podunkville,
    bohunk, poverty-ridden low-class, back-end of beyond, rural know-
    nothing nowhere.

And I have ordered expensive shoes on-line to try and make up the
    difference.
And on the phone I change my accent with telemarketers and pollsters
    I have no reason to impress.
I have lowered my voice and ducked my head and grinned and felt
    murderous when, in other places, I speak and people look at me with
    surprise and disappointment and ask me where I'm from,
    as if the mother ship has landed, as if I've arrived with a pone of
    cornbread in my hand and lice in my hair and an ignorant, dullard
    brain in my head.

America, my students
who don't believe there's a class division, a pecking order, a hard road
    ahead,
who disdain the housekeepers in their dorms,
who make fun of poor whites, trailer trash, rednecks,
who go on mission trips to *impoverished* places like Haiti and India and
    rural China,
who don't recognize the sounds of their own prejudice any more than
    they recognize
    their own poor grammar, look at me with confusion when I tell them:
You sweet naive children, dear darlings for whom I've sacrificed a
    different kind of life, you are and always will be somebody's
    hillbilly.

America, Appalachia gave up nothing to you in its timber, its coal, its
    dignity, nothing compared to giving you its children, whom you will
    begrudgingly agree to take, if they straighten up and dumb down
    their ways, and even out their hick accents, and smarten up their acts,

and blend and homogenize.

America, I'm not here like my ancestors who made charcoal and pig iron
that started this country.
I'm not here digging out coal or zinc, or lobbying for or against strip-
mining or mountain-top coal removal, although I know you are still
up to your tricks.
I'm not picketing your coal-burning plants that muddy up my air while
you breathe clean, or protesting the hydroelectric dams that broke
our rivers.
I'm not logging any forests—like my granddaddy who built your
furniture.
I'm not raising any tobacco—like my daddy did—to put me through
school.
I'm not making quilts or weaving baskets—like my grandmothers did—
for you to buy on vacation.
I'm not preaching Jesus or hellfire.
I'm not handling any snakes or distilling moonshine (which you like to
read about).
I'm not playing a banjo or fiddle or singing any godforsaken, melancholy
ballad.

What I'm doing is way more dangerous, teaching a bunch of kids:
that the brains God gave them are for something besides Vols football
stats and NASCAR drivers' numbers,
that they grew up on the front lines, set by the Deists and the Calvinists
we sprang from right here, where freedom of and from religion are
still put to the test;
that faith and evolution coexist with God the Father and Jesus the Son,
Amen;
that we've been called backward and barbarian and heathen and simple
and quaint and lazy and uncivilized—a hybrid, mongrel, monstrous
underclass;
that they get to decide what to call themselves next;
that they have a choice.
But that to misplace their commas and semi-colons might create a bigger
dividing line than they can imagine,
that to avoid sentence fragments and agreement errors might save their
lives,
that they should learn not to say, "I seen him go over the ridge," or
"when we've went to town," or "my mama and them says to tell you
hey;"
and that they should never dare correct their grandparents or parents

for saying the same.

I spend hours marking their every error I can catch, using all the energy I
    have without giving away how truly terrified I am for them,
    of the possible dead-end hourly pay and time-clock-punching that's
    historically, nearly unavoidably theirs,
of the threat of a vertical backyard behind the double-wide trailer of their
    futures, or
of a future they might spend like me, a traitor, teaching the next
    generation to leave.
America, I'm getting them as ready as I can to climb onto that airplane or
    Greyhound, or into their daddy's Hemi pickup, or to hitch a ride with
    somebody eastbound, westbound, northbound, to put on their boots
    and take up their beds and U-Haul it out of here.
America, I'm putting my hillbilly shoulder to the wheel.

KB Ballentine

Of Roots

Light lingers
on this leaf,
that patch of grass,
cardinal insisting
from inside
the honeysuckle bush.
This is the moment
to be still.
Allow the sound
of chimes and crows
to lick your skin,
sink in
where your blood
rivers to your heart.
Is this the joy,
the peace we have
when we lean
into the sun?
See the echo of moon,
the blue above
eclipsing the stars
that sing
whether we see them
or not?
Bees nuzzle
clover, ants tracing
peonies, sweetness
tugged underground.
And now the grumble
of motors, of brakes
coughs through,
a siren screeching past.
Even so, the pines rise,
maples sugaring
both bud and root.
The most important labor
taking place
somewhere
out of sight.

KB Ballentine

Falling Between

This is how it begins:

    leaves brushed with yellow in the trees,
  a hawk's shadow masking parched roses,
whispers of rain ghosting the ridge.

    Figs bruise the yard—
sticky patches abandoned by all but bees and ants.

Wrapped in these last warm days,
    we walk through wood-light,
  the rumor of autumn closing in,
mountain laurel and ferns curling in blistered clusters.

    Fewer bird calls in the sweetgum, the cedar,
  silence surging like a drowning tide
though two deer lift their heads through leaf-gold.

    We wind our way past tulip trees, purple hearts
  tucked deep against the coming chill,
lose the light as gray sweeps overhead,
    mist pearling into firmer drops.

    One last breath before heading inside,
the taste of leaving on our tongues.

Jessica D. Thompson

The Blacksmith
—for Martin

Before a hammer meets an anvil,
there is a pause midair

and time is suspended.
He forged horseshoes in a fire

built each day before sunrise.
Before bed, he would brush

her hair one hundred strokes.
I never saw such tenderness.

He must have thought of water
falling from a sun-struck cliff.

He must have thought of rose
petals floating in a rain barrel.

He must have thought he heard
a whisper of wings—

a sparrow

singing in the palm of his hand.

Cynthia Shutts

First Family

Some things will never change. Tar paper shacks scatter the green hillside as if they are hidden gnomes or fairies peeking out into the valley below. They do not want to be found, so the metal monster whizzes past them unflinching. It lurches up the track until suddenly the houses appear in tiny lines, tiny rows of straight white clapboard become a town with a mountainside behind it. Next small, curvy creeks become two rivers that merge, and I am home.

I remember this place because it was once a shackle, an unwanted tattoo that appeared with a tempered teenage declaration of rebellion. I will never come back here until everyone I know has died or moved away. As the farm expanded, it burned or shoveled under every rabbit hutch, charring my sense of security.

Now, I feel guilty about that threat because the phone call came. The one you always wait for, for which you are never really prepared. My sister phoned because our mother was now in hospice again. If I wanted to see her, it needed to be soon, or now. Especially because she wasn't in town and I could probably get there before she could.

I packed up my entire life for yet a third time and headed toward the Mid-Ohio Valley.

We are always preached at to forgive even if you can't forget, and I could barely do either after my first two attempts at intervention with mother.

The first time, my sister called and described mom's behavior, ending the phone call with "You are the eldest. Do something!"

I packed my entire life up in Kansas City, said "goodbye" to dear friends and a woman I had just started to love, and moved home with my young son.

As badly as I wanted to shelter him from my mother's shenanigans and alcoholic behavior, another part of me dared myself to give him just enough of a taste to scare him away from booze.

I arrived to find my mother curled up on her couch like an unwashed fetus, unable to stand or move or feed herself. It only took two late-night hallucinatory calls from her reporting that some man was breaking in her bedroom window for me to put my "DO SOMETHING" into action.

I went to mom's apartment on the second break-in attempt to find her down on the carpet in her nightie, unable to get back onto the couch. I think she had been making her best effort to crawl to the toilet. At that moment, my first thought as I paused in her doorway not quite sure what to do, I asked myself, "Is this what you were afraid of for thirty-five years?"

A second later, my gut jolted. It was as if I had kicked in the doorway, and I went to lift Mother off the floor. I could put her on her couch and continue enabling her, or I could walk her to the car and drive to detox.

As soon as I strapped into my seatbelt, a strange feeling came over me, and I could hear in my head, Tyne Daly, as Mary Beth Lacey telling me, "It was a good collar, Chris."

That's when I felt relief, knowing I had dismantled the perp from her whiskey bottle (gun) and walked her to my car for the trip to detox.

A few weeks later, our entire family was compliant with her needs and the hospital's instructions. Everyone except Mom.

She began a nail in her coffin from which I barely recovered. It started with the statement, "A.A. meetings are boring. Those people talk about how broken they are and the crap they put everyone through, and it is too depressing to go." The final strike to the nail was her insistent, "Nobody has ever done anything for me."

Livid was minimal. I am not sure what to call the way my brain responded. I completely lost all sanity for a moment, because there was no use to argue with a drunk. I decided at that moment to begin doing things in the neighborhood that appealed to me and would help my son and me to thrive. As soon as the money was raised to return to Kansas City, I would be putting a thousand miles between us. Since clearly, I had done nothing to help her, and further, you can't help someone who does not want help. She just wasn't ready. Out of jail on a technicality. She wasn't read her rights, SO she claimed. I even went to a therapist for advice, having just finished the Kate Millett book *The Loony Bin Trip*.

I wanted someone to see my mother was as crazy as we knew she was. My siblings and I sat her down in the family home that she was about to lose and threatened, "Stop this now! Or you will never see your grandchildren again. We can't risk losing our children to your bad behavior." I screamed at her in a decibel that made my throat break and bleed a little.

Millett's family kept committing her to psychiatric services when she did not agree with them politically or donated money to a cause of which they did not approve. She ended up on Lithium and labeled crazy. Any time Kate attempted to offer a passionate opinion after that, she was labeled incapable.

The therapist was not uncaring to my plea, but firmly barked back, "That BOOK is now the reason you can't just have her committed involuntarily."

The metaphorical coffin slammed, so I began to raise money to leave. I kept a safe distance for almost two years and then returned to the Midwest, attempting to regain my previous life. Friends would periodically ask how my mother was doing, and I would scowl in response and snarkily reply, "Just waiting for the undertaker to call."

A dozen years passed, and I decided to bring Ben home over Memorial Day to see the other family, and grandparents, adding, "We will stop and see Gammy if there is time."

I wasn't lying to him, but I was dreading the possibility of having to see her. I had heard nothing good about her living arrangement, and as hard as it was to believe, I finally told myself, I don't have to stay long, but I knew Ben really did want to see her.

Everything was worse than I imagined and five times worse than I had been told. Almost every family member had pulled out of her life because she had four people living with her. Two women and two men had relegated her to sleeping on the couch in a teddy bear nightie and an adult diaper. They changed her on the couch, and said they were there "TO TAKE CARE OF HER?" The pile of used Depends and ashes on the floor at one end of the couch told a different tale.

Apparently, her housemates cooked candy at night and sold it in a doctor's office parking lot to supplement their low social security incomes. CANDY! She said she was glad when they left for the day because whatever they cooked did not smell very good, and she wasn't mobile enough to get to the kitchen and turn off the stove. Maybe they were letting it burn. None of her Christmas candy ever smelled like that!

Clearly, my mother was housing a shake and bake operation and couldn't tell Meth or Cocaine from Christmas fudge.

The photographs were proof that she was in the end stages of liver failure and yellowed with jaundice. I could not become her legal guardian due to my out of state resident status. My sister agreed to become the guardian if I would wrangle the paperwork.

My brother appeared with gun and badge in hand to exterminate the four roach-like loiterers, who claimed they paid rent. While mom was in detox, my partner did a complete inventory of all her belongings. We prepared to move in with her when she came home from the hospital this time.

We cooked for her, but she wouldn't eat. We invited her out, but she refused to go. Shortly after my son's sixteenth birthday on Thanksgiving, she started a tantrum that did not end until Christmas Eve. She threw us out with nowhere to go. I was officially done.

That had been five years ago. There were one or two strokes and a heart attack or two in the interim. Then there were a couple of breakouts. When Granny and Mom's sister, Judy, didn't like the nursing home she was in, they broke her out. A couple of weeks later, she would be back in her trailer, sloshed, and calling 911 three times a day. Done. I literally was waiting for the undertaker to call.

Sadly, I knew more about death than the average human. A nurse for thirty-five years, my partner spent a good portion of that in geriatrics and hospice. The moment people feel like they are in cancer remission, and Jesus has healed them, they have roughly two weeks left. It's called the "rally." Unbeknownst to my sister and brother, my mother was about to "rally."

I didn't know what I would see after five years away. Mom had been hospitalized with strokes, heart attacks, and lung cancer. Alcoholism was now minimal. I didn't even know if she would talk to me since our last meeting had been the Christmas Eve brawl. Technically, she was sick enough to not even know who I was.

Cautiously, I peered into the room. Sitting on the edge of her bed, Mom looked up, saw me, and the first thing she said was, "My baby is here."

She hadn't remained mad at all, just thought I was in Kansas collecting taxes, and raising belligerent teenage boys.

We sat for a couple of hours talking, and then out of the blue, she said, "I know you still feel lost. I think it is time for you to find your people."

I am not sure even now what was harder to hear. Mother was making her last request, and her last request wasn't even for her. It was for me.

Lana Austin

In Search of the Wild Dulcimer
for Jean Ritchie

I need something pure
            with both a newborn

and dying woman's cry,
            each connected to a single

line of light, one
            at its beginning and another

at its end. Or is it more
            of a curving river or a circle

of sound, unadulterated tremolo:
            the dulcimer. I've found

Jean Ritchie, her ballad
            matching her wild mountain

instrument, the one she made
            by hand, the one born out of her

Scots-Irish Kentucky roots,
            a simple incandescent strand

I somehow still hear
            without much effort,

despite my rising deafness,
            her voice and dulcimer

a single aural finger that points
            to me. It grows both lonesome

and tremblingly full,
            a rain cloud about to pour out

a host of voices from sky
            to ground and back again.

Lana Austin

Amulet of Sound
for Ricky Skaggs

Your hands become hummingbirds
flitting into a blur as your body shelters
not just a mandolin, but an amulet of sound.
Your fingers usher me through aural catacombs–

resplendent caverns of song—that defy dark,
until I have forgotten that my brother has forgotten
how to sing, his memory now immured,
his drunk tongue entombed.

Natalie Kimbell

I Am a River of Stories

I am a river of stories
      passing fluid, mother to daughter
distinct like the sound of skipping stones,
      skimming across transparent pools of eternity.

In story, I am the collected voices of my kin
      who rise above and below the flood line.
I am the keeper of salacious secrets
      and callous dispatches.

In story, I raise my distant cousin Alifair
      whose husband in 1895 demanded she ride a horse
until she aborted a baby he didn't mean to give her.
      He was deemed guilt-free, before the corpses were cold.

In story, I row the bold whispers between women
      of Silvaney, who my Grandma declared a witch.
A woman who wed my Uncle Irving using spells
      lacing his drinks with a sliver of her cum.

In story, I continue our saga in rippling patterns
      repeating my Grandmother's
and my mother's and my own history,
      of loving men who would not stay.

In story, I deliver back family from the river Styx,
      baptizing them in my breath
lifting them up out of the shallows
      making them current.
I am a river of stories.

Barbara Sabol

I Washed into the World
—May 31, 1939

I washed into the world on the sodden mattress
that floated my pregnant mother
into the second story window of Alma Hall.

In the pitch blackness of that shivering night
I am told the contractions came on full-force.
Her screams of pain likely drowned out

by the shouts and sobs of two hundred some
terrified and injured in that same room; by the wind's
sharp howl, the incessant crash and splinter
of buildings, bodies, God-knows-what outside.

Standing here now in front of Alma Hall, I gaze up
to the second-floor watermark, the elliptical arches
like raised eyebrows, and conjure some primal memory

of being delivered from one floating world
into another by a doctor with three broken ribs
while eighteen feet of water sloshed at the sill.

I am told that the Presbyterian Church steeple
split the wave in two, sending the wall of water
to either side of the hall, sparing all but one
of those sheltered inside.

Over the years I have pieced together
what I've been told about the night of my birth
when a flood leveled the city of Johnstown.
A patchwork of story and surmise.

On my 50th birthday I've returned to see the lanterns
lit along the stone bridge, to visit the ground
where my ancestral home folded into itself
like an envelope

I have come to visit the plot of the unknown drowned
at Grandview Cemetery, and run my hand along the arc
of every blank stone.

Randi Ward
Muse

Kelli Hansel Haywood

Roadside Sale

Glass trinkets on fold out tables
reflect sun.
A few from his wife's curio.
Sometimes he finds himself
able to remove a piece or two,
feels her eyes still watching him,
like the cooper's hawk
that circles the chicken yard.
He keeps meaning to shoot that thing.

Sun-tanned women more broken
than they let on
circle the tables.
Flip flopped, tank topped, pink toenailed.
Betsy would say dressed too young
for their age.

"How much for this beveled glass?" one asks.
He thinks, but can't remember
how much was give for it.
"What you got on the fiestaware?" another asks,
before he can answer the first.

It's hard to see them walk off
with her pretties.
She'd get him, because he knows he let
those women get away with a steal.
But, he can't stand sitting at the house.

It's quiet.
One can only watch Gunsmoke
so many times.
The new guy on Price is Right
looks out of place.
No Bob Barker.

He rearranges the pieces
on the table to fill in the holes.
Maybe next Saturday he'll bring

a few of the rifles from his cabinet.
Sits down in Betsy's lawnchair
to finish his chicken biscuit
from the Kwik Mart.
Coffee's done cooled off,
even with this blazing sun.
Wasn't any count no way.

Libby Falk Jones

Appalachian Ghazal

"The ground's generosity takes in our compost and grows beauty,"
Rumi writes. He must have dreamed Kentucky's wild spring beauty:

stands of red and yellow columbine by barbed wire fences, pale thistles
dotting mustard fields, mayapple umbrellas quivering in rain, the beauti-

ful abandon of roadside morning glories, daisies winking white
in morning sun. Oh, color's often at the heart of beauty:

at dusk, when Owlsley Lake runs red and five black ducks
glide toward the shore, the camera captures beauty.

Perhaps the form's the key: intricacies of hosta, clematis vines,
the shagbark hickory's skin, the dogwood's curl: geometries of beauty.

There's nature's glory, never spent, what Hopkins called the "dearest
freshness deep down things"—a truth to live for: hidden beauty.

And you, my love, who cycles by my side, who calls me
love, what I have ever known with you is beauty.

Natalie Sypolt

Eleven to Seven

I wake up in a cold sweat, heart beating fast and hands clamped so tight into fists that half moon shaped marks are left on my palms. Enis has been on midnights, and I don't sleep right anymore. My internal clock ticks off beat. The kids are unphased by his comings and goings, still go to bed and get up for school like they always have, but I feel constantly off kilter, even on nights when he is home.

The dream hadn't felt like a dream. It was a flash that I felt in my body—a heaviness that made me know it was real.

The men were working on the catwalk.

The man was going over—falling or jumping—in the giant bowl full of fire.

I've never been inside the mill where Enis works, but just the same I knew that's where I was, just as strong as I knew the man who went into that vat of molten steel was Enis.

Even in the dream, I could not tell if he had fallen or if he had jumped.

It is mid-day, the kids at school and Enis, not in bed beside me, but someplace else, maybe downstairs or outside working on the car. His clock is off too and I worried about him being too tired at work, so tired that he won't pay attention, won't be careful.

Sleeping in the bright light of day feels unnatural, but when the wave of exhaustion comes over me, I have to climb in the bed.

Some days, Enis will lay back down with me, wake me up with a cold hand against my belly. Half awake and half asleep, I'll roll into him. "Jude," he'll say close into my ear.

When I wake up again, he'll be really and truly gone, in the shower, ready for work.

And I will be here, in this house all alone again. I'll clean the kitchen floor, get down on my hands and knees and scrub the spaces between the tiles until my skin is red and raw. I watched Mom do it, too, sweeping and mopping and scrubbing, and then Dad and the boys would come in, tracking whatever mud and grease and dog shit, and she'd just get out the bucket and do it all over again.

When she cooked the dinner for all them people, the men'd eat first and me and her would stand back and wait, eat what was left. I used to think how if it were me, I'd keep back something, hide the best piece of meat or a sweet little morsel for myself. She never did though.

Everything in this house is narrow and dark. I never feel like I can truly see his face, but up in our bedroom where the windows are tall and let in the daylight. The house is old, a row house attached to other old narrow houses on each side, just one little plot of dirt out front by the cement walkway where I try to plant a few flowers in the springtime, anything for a little light. Last summer, I planted some pineys that I got from home and they grew up tall like they do, and then when they bloomed their heads were so heavy they drooped down. I love them because they are both beautiful and sad all at the same time.

The neighbor lady couldn't stop talking about my flowers, like they ain't never seen a flower in Pittsburgh before, and kept bragging on me. She even got the lady from a couple houses down the way to look at them, and I told her they weren't anything, really. I just threw some bulbs in some dirt. Wasn't anything special at all.

Some days my whole body aches to be home, down in the holler, held in by those mountains.

I can't get the dream out of my head. That man falling from the catwalk, disappearing into that giant drum of molten steel. Them bosses, they probably wouldn't even stop work long enough to try and find that man—if there was anything to find—and he'd end up in some building's skeleton.

I ask Enis not to go to work and he laughs at me. I say to him, "Please stay, just tonight." I never have asked him to miss work. I know there are boys always in line for any job at the mills, but I ask, just this once.

We are in the hallway in the darkening evening. He's about to leave out for his 11-7 shift. He's carrying that dinged tin lunch pail and his silver J&L id tag is pinned to his shirt. I've had that in my hands so many times, I know the badge is thin metal that will not hold up in that hot, hot liquid steel.

"I don't want you to go to work," I say.

"I got to," he says. "You want to eat, don't you?"

"In the dream, you were falling into one of the big vats."

Him: Bullshit.

Me: Stay home.

Him: Nothing will happen. Nothing ever happens.

Me: But sometimes my feelings are true. Sometimes—my dreams—

Him: I ain't losing my job because of you and your dreams.

I sit up all night, watching Johnny Carson and then the late movie, and then the stars and stripes sign off.

In my head, I see the orange sun coming up in the holler, the whole sky catching on fire the way it does on some of those cold mornings. It's early March, but in West Virginia, there will still be snow, and that burning sky will reflect up off of it, making the whole world glow. I miss home so bad that tears sting my eyes, and I wonder how we will ever get there.

What will it be like to know for sure that I have lost Enis? How much can a person lose in her life and still get on?

At 7:30, I don't hear the bolt turn on the front door and then the sound of Enis' boots, slow and heavy in the hall like I should. When I still don't hear it by 8:00, I am sure he is dead.

Finally, at a quarter after 9, the door creaks open and he comes in, looking so tired and worn that no sleep could help him.

I stand up in the chair I'm sitting in, just unfolding my legs underneath me instead of putting them on the cold floor. I reach my arms out to him like a little child and wait for him to come to me.

"You're late," I say into his neck as he lifts me, holds me so close like he is trying to pull me into himself.

"There was an accident," he says, "John Defazio."

In my head, Enis falling off the catwalk into the tub of liquid steel changes and it's John's dark head I see.

"I was only a few feet behind him," Enis is saying into my hair. "I saw him go, but there wasn't nothing I could do."

"I know," I say.

I'm lying in the bed again, and Enis is sleeping deep, stretched out next to me. This is the room in our dark, narrow house that is full of light, and the sun comes in the window, across the floor, and onto the bed in a slant. I want it to make me happy, but it is thin light, not the golden light of home. I need the feel of that wind pushing thick through the trees and against my face. In the holler, there is a moon at night, and stars that you can see instead of just knowing they're there behind the smoke from the mills and lights from the city.

Maybe now we will leave this place and start again.

But today Enis has to sleep because we need to have dinner soon, and then he has to leave out of here, back to the mill, back for the 11 to 7 shift.

Laura Sweeney

Prayer For The Woman In The Coop
(*after The Short List of Certainty by Lois Roma Deeley*)

Let her remember the smell of bugspray
    and unbrushed teeth
        the taste of jarred applesauce, mixed nuts
           and canned pineapple juice

let her remember the way the spider shimmies up a thread
    while the large black ant crawls
        on the wooden plank and two white caterpillars
           sunbathe on the deck

can't you picture this woman sitting in a blue lawn chair
    next to a gallon of water next to an ax she has no use for
        how this woman spots a wild turkey
           strutting up the road shaking its feathers
              turning into the summer grass

can't you picture this woman on the coop's deck
    enjoying the green green green of the thousand Copper Mountain
        trees or the geckos that leap limb to limb
           can't you picture her breathing in the butterflied
           and cardinaled air

think not of the ticks she pulls off herself and her dog
    how her dog growls bares her teeth

think not of her back injury how she's carried her cooler
    up and down the gravel path
        stocked with mozz, pico de gallo, baguette, seltzer water

nor of the girls who wander into the woods alone
    against all warnings

think only of the breeze that wafts across her deck
    the whirred white noise of her battteried fans
        think of the promise she made to herself
           like saving for a tiny house

bless this woman who extricated herself
    though she doesn't know how to chop wood
        she knows what it means to go to the woods
            to woodshed a life onto the page

let her go forth from here down the gravel path
    doxie beside her
        where the wild turkey stood
            towards the barbed wire fence

and the unruly road
    toward all the uncertainty that lies ahead
a wild song beating in her breast

Virginia Parfitt

My mother's hands

My sister has my mother's hands
they say, and I have her nose.

Part and parcel, she has been prised apart,
re-appropriated, given new life
for new use, on other bodies.

How would she feel about this I wonder
to know that she lives on;
a piece here, a part there
her cheekbones on a niece
her eyebrows on a grandchild.

Does someone get
the belly laugh,
and the far-away look
in faded blue eyes?
Who gets the Ivy league vocabulary
that belies a 7th grade education?

And who receives the moribund heart,
the pre-diabetes, the
end stage renal disease?
Who is the lucky recipient of the womb
that birthed a baker's dozen, one of which was me?

Would she scoff, modestly,
claim that even if they were her features,
they surely look better on someone else?

Or would she smile her crooked smile,
that my daughter has,
to know that she lives on,
life after death?

I think she'd be happy,
in an absurd sort of way;
she'd nod her snowy head, slowly,
look carefully at the new baby,

through rheumy eyes,
and say,
"why, she's the spitting image
of my grandmother."

Cat Pleska

Wash Me Clean . . .

Norma sat the baby in a clawfoot tub. Immediately, chubby hands splashed the water. Kneeling beside the tub, she soaped the baby's belly with a washrag then moved to her back. She lifted each splashing hand and massaged suds around the fingers. Rinsing the soap from the rag, she wrung the water out and cleaned the baby's face, neck, and ears then scruffed up sparse hair tufts. The baby was nearly bald when born, but now, six months later, she sported only "peach fuzz" as Norma called it. Her older sister, Jean, pretended insult. "My daughter does so have hair!"

She grabbed the slippery baby and stood her up, scrubbed her bottom and legs. Norma clicked her tongue and said, "I forgot your towel. I'll be right back." She left the baby, newly able to sit, and stepped into the hall to the linen closet. She rummaged in the meager stack for the softest towel. Her sister didn't have much. At only 18, she came into the marriage with the clothes on her back. In the year and half since, not much was added, save her child. Norma selected a towel and closed the closet door.

She turned at the bathroom doorway and a jolt roiled through her body at the sight—an empty tub. She dropped the towel and hurried closer. The baby lay submerged, staring wide-eyed up at the ceiling. No bubbles, no movement.

Norma reached in and jerked her up, peering at her face. Then she shook her, gently. "Breathe! Breathe!" She begged.

The baby coughed water. She blinked and the wails began. Norma brought her fully out of the tub, grabbed the towel, and wrapped her. She pulled her close. "Shhhh. Shhhh. You're okay. You're all right." Sobs eased, sleepy eyes blinking. Looking for signs of steady breathing, or blue around the mouth, relief flooded Norma's body—a healthy pink baby glowed in her arms.

In the bedroom, she wrangled on a diaper and dressed her in a sleeper, placing her in the crib. The baby kicked, but soon her eyes closed. In her sleep, she smiled, which means she was listening to angels.

Walking to the living room, Norma paced, muttering. "Oh my God! Jean will kill me! What do I know about babies? I'm just 17. She shouldn't have left her with me. . . . She is all Jean has. . . . She will never forgive me."

Norma sat down on the couch and put her head in her hands. Then she straightened and inhaled deeply. "I won't tell her," she said out loud. She needed to calm down, or keep busy, she didn't know. But she walked to the kitchen. Grabbing an aluminum coffee pot, she filled it with water, dumped coffee in the metal basket, and pressed on the lid. Setting it on the stove, she searched for a match. She turned the knob to the stove's burner, lit the match, and the flame caught.

She stared out the window noting the neighbors' houses. She had no phone. *Which one would she run to if the baby had not breathed? How do you call the police, or an ambulance?*

Sipping the strong coffee from her mug, she swallowed hard, and said aloud: "Jean will never know."

Decades later, I was visiting my aunt Norma for Christmas. At 80, she was the closest person I had as a mother figure since my mom had died 16 years earlier. The two had been close, even inventing a language when they were children only they spoke and understood.

I dreaded the eight-hour drive to visit, but I did because my aunt is the last person in my life to love me unconditionally, as my mother had. I felt the same way about her—I would forgive her anything.

One day, on that visit, Norma and I were talking. I don't remember about what, but she turned to me and said, "I nearly drowned you when you were a baby."

Startled, I finally managed to say, "Mom never told me."

"No, she didn't. She never knew. Here's exactly what happened. Every bit of it." She settled in her chair and looked to the distance and began.

As I listened, my hand crept up to my neck, and then cradled my chin. I felt as if I'd slipped away from my anchor, set adrift on a rough sea.

Beth Wolfe

Postponed

My dreams, my works, must wait
says the world.
They must wait for such a
time that all dust has been
swept. All dishes cleared. All
socks matched. They must
wait until all bills are
paid, until there is enough in the
bank for a thousand rainy days.
My dreams must not
threaten the dreams
of those whom history has
never made wait
for fulfillment.
My works—mine—the world
demands be
deferred in submission to the
duty the world
presumes for me. My dreams,
my works, must wait says the
world. Wait for
permission I do not
seek from a
world to whom
I do not
answer.

Eileen Mouyard

snow coming down

continues to leave me
fascinated
it's blanketing silence
and ability to slow time
in an instant—
a fairy godmother finger-snap
from the clouds
who doesn't look out the window
and say out loud
"it's snowing"
i see a person pressed to a window
in a home below my street
gray puffy smoke swirls above the chimney
where a fire
warms her walls
but the floors stay cold, i bet
i think of how i hope
she has wool socks
sipping my coffee i whisper
wordlessly
"cheers, anonymous neighbor
how do the lights look
from where you are?"
from where i am
it is a postcard
of fog and dampness
of rust and yellow-green-gold glow
of homes keeping people
out of the cold
but not away from their windows
not away from remembering where they are—
this is what we meant
i think
when we named the word
hope

Bonnie Proudfoot

What Doesn't Kill You

Weeks after the surgery, after the sling
came off and after the stitches started
to dissolve in layers of epidermis
under her breast, the radiation began.
After that, chemo for a year,
as soon as she can take it. What
doesn't kill you makes you stronger
say some, probably folks who never watched
this kind of cure or watched a body
be ravaged like this. We live
in cancer valley, teflon in the water,
cattle belly up, no one wants to admit
exactly how all this shit got into
everything, but now it is seeping
into the pores of friends and family,
and hurt expands from the streams
to the mountain tops where we really see
the scene of the crime. Giant drills buzz
in the night and someone's tap drips poison.
It is a growing game of chance, but we
are playing with a rigged deck,
the dealer holds all the cards.
On the way to Fairmont, leaves fall
and Rt. 50 burns, license plates
from Texas and Oklahoma blast past.
Under the earth, the ground shakes,
just beyond, the land is pocked and cracked
like a scar. What doesn't make you stronger
can also kill you. It will not be pretty.
At the Shell station, everyone mentions
the pipeline as if it is the yellow brick road.

Bonnie Proudfoot

Doves

Outside my window this morning, snow
piles up on porch rails and trees,
the only motion is a pair of doves perched
under the eaves, thin black beaks, clay-colored,
round heads pressing together like a valentine,
their coo-coo-coo ocarina calls set off against
a backdrop of silent snowflakes. If they're
the same pair as the last 3 years, they arrived
early, mid-February instead of April, but maybe
this year they're trying to get it right.

They've had a run of bad luck, no postman-stork
delivering baby doves, instead clutches of eggs
that refuse to hatch or tiny naked chicks that don't
make it. Long after the wrens, flycatchers
and robins build their nests, dart to the lawn
and head back to a cluster of open mouths,
after those other fledglings stand in a little bird
conga line on the porch railings and work up
the nerve to take first flights, this pair of doves
is still in phase one, trading shifts, nest guarding,
egg sitting, unflinching and inscrutable as buddhas
their ruby eyes meet mine as I head outside.

I could climb a stepladder, chase them off,
clean out the nest, but I can't bring myself
to break it to them. Do you know what I mean?
Maybe they don't see the writing on the wall,
or they could care less about the other birds,
they stay with the thing that matters most,
and I wish I was more like that, after all,
there isn't a day that doesn't have its share
of glaring headlines, dire conclusions, so many
wrecking balls aimed at every plan. Even today,
disaster hangs like the wind-chill factor, and here
they are, innocent optimists with work to do,
all hopes and feathers and dreams.

Melissa Helton

This Split Road in the Green Forest

reminds me of my teenager's raised peace-sign fingers
when I turned to look at her on our evening walk yesterday,
which reminds me of my raised peace sign fingers
in the photo taken when I met her father back in the 90s,
which reminds me that she is almost the age I was then,
which reminds me of a billion things I don't want
her to experience, which reminds me of a wooden
crate in a dusty attic in a movie I saw and hated,
which reminds me of the creaking sound of old brass hinges,
which reminds me of the creaking I feel deep in my knee,
like plastic on plastic, when I walk up the stairs,
which reminds me of falling on the dark ice before
the brick house, drunk and having broken my vows,
which reminds me of this split road in the green forest,
which reminds me of gravel under summer-thick soles in childhood,
which reminds me of a deck stacked against me,
which reminds me of this idea of god everyone talks about,
the Deck-Stacker, which reminds me of prepubescent crawling
under the pews on a Wednesday evening while mother practiced the organ
and rainbow light streaked me between the darknesses.

Melissa Helton

Give Me Poems

Poems like sourwood honey, sit
glowing, jarred in the quiet pantry,
waiting on a special occasion. Poems
like a vernacular fever burning
the tongues of the foreign, the domestic,
the weary traveler, patient
zero of the coming epidemic.
Poems like a neck, which swivels
the head this way and that,
in whatever direction it wants
the head to see. Poems like frost
glitter on the crocus. Poems like thrush
in the mouths of babies and AIDS patients.
Poems like werewolves, ancient
fear told by drunk men to delight
and terrify kids, filling dreams
with rabid howls. Poems like lice
alight on the child, hard to rid,
all the house bedding in boiling water,
contagious when we put
our heads together. Poems like a line
that became a quote that became a battlecry
that became a bumpersticker that became a meme
making fun of old people.
Poems like fennel soup on the stove,
steaming off its telltale fragrance, calling
to the table you, who hate it,
but are hungry enough to eat.

Angelyn DeBord
Three Friends

Jessica Manack

Let The Record Show

My mother's father, Bernard, was my just-missed train. I arrived 11 days after my due date and he died 6 days before I was born. That's some sad math. Somewhere around the infrequent, elusive February 29, which did occur that year, we might have shaken hands. But it was not to be. I wouldn't have been born at all, if my father's mother had had her way. She knew that my parents hadn't meant to conceive a child and were not prepared, that my father was not an adult yet, couldn't even take care of himself. She encouraged my mother to terminate. But my mother was stubborn: young, but sure of her path.

Since I was short a grandfather on the Serbian side, great-aunts and great-uncles proved invaluable, a link to the old country, faces to find bits of myself in, evidence of how a furrowed brow could catch the light just like mine.

My mother hadn't known all of her grandparents, either. Bernard's mother, her grandmother, Petra, had died when she was very small. But the story lived on: Petra keeled over in church, right in the middle of a service one Sunday. People would recount this with a definitive air, as though the rest of the story wrote itself. *She was already halfway home.* Without the science we have today, the explanations that stuck were the ones easiest to latch on to. *God needed another angel. What better way to go?*

Unfortunate losses were a theme on that side of our family. Petra's daughter Mildred, my great-aunt, had also died too soon, at age 17. Perhaps Bernard didn't ever expect to make it past his 50s. Maybe he never expected to meet his grandchildren. Maybe his side of the family didn't have the best genes, or the best luck.

These stories occupied my mind as I prepared to have my own child. As my due date came and went, the baby happy to stay where he was, I kept myself busy during those frigid winter days by working on my family tree.

I poked around in online databases, typing in the names of people I had always wanted to know more about. I found Petra's death certificate, bearing the details in black-and-white type: *St. George Church, 10th Street, Midland, PA. Acute coronary occlusion.*

Mildred was another. First, I found her obituary, which stated that she too died on a Sunday afternoon, after a week's illness. This didn't correspond to what I'd always been told, though: that she had died of a heart attack like her mother. I wanted to find out more.

Doing a search for Mildred on another site produced a death certificate. I opened it up, quickly scanning past what I already knew—

Parents: Michael and Petra. Parents' place of birth: Jugo Slavia—to see if there was any new information. And there was. A cause of death: *Septicemia, peritonitis, and meningitis following self-induced abortion (two and a half months' gestation).* She was 17 years, 7 months and 6 days old, born in America, the first child of her family to be born in this new land.

I don't know—*can't* know—all the details, her whys. It's tempting to let the mind wander. It was the middle of the Great Depression. 1934. She was the eldest of five children. Old enough to maintain a household. A woman, not likely to earn a good wage. So she was married off, and her child would have been legitimate, at least. But there could be any number of reasons why she thought she couldn't have this baby, why being pregnant any longer seemed untenable.

We could imagine infinite whys, or we could accept that one has one's reason. Do we need to know anyone's reason? What does a person get to keep to themselves? My mother is alive and we speak nearly daily. But I have never felt it my place to ask her why, though she shared with me the fact that she chose to have me despite opposition: Was it as simple as believing that the life inside you deserved its chance? Did you think you could fit my nuclear bomb of a father into a nuclear family? Were you bored? Did you want a doll? Did you want a friend?

Somehow, talking about those who can't talk back was easier. I asked my mother again, the other day, as we discussed the ailments of various aging family members, to remind me how her Aunt Mildred had died. "Heart attack," she answered quickly.

I told her that that wasn't true. I told her what I had learned. She was incredulous, asking for more details.

"What? It just says *that*? Right there on the paper? They wrote all that out? That she did it herself?" She does what I did, tries to fill in the unfillable blanks. "And what else? She didn't love the guy?"

My son does the same thing, asks me to find information that doesn't exist. *Show me a picture of a purple dragon eating a pink banana on a green bulldozer. Look for it on the computer.* I know it's hard to grasp, sometimes, the amount of information we have access to, so it's easy to start thinking that we might be able to know the unknowable.

I explain to her that, yes, it's all written there, in those words, a reminder of how little control we have over our story once it ends. I show her the file as she takes in the fact that she never got to know her aunt, but that she might have had another cousin, too. Maybe she wonders, like I did, if Petra died of a broken heart.

Something about being the one to tell my mother this feels wrong. She should be the one educating me about our history. I don't know the protocol for comforting her. I don't like being responsible for giving her sad news about people I never met, people I never mourned. My mother is already so averse to learning anything from me. I try to share recipes, to give her advice on her investments, explain the difference between a Roth and a 401(k), but she doesn't want to hear it. Isn't this why people have kids? To have a hand to hold as we are propelled into The Future?

She doesn't like that my knowledge on some topics has surpassed hers. I wonder if I misunderstood the directive to learn, to soak up education like a sponge. Or, should I have shielded my mother from this knowledge? She hadn't sought it out. She hadn't known it was there to seek.

It's uncomfortable to think about the things we thought we were doing in secret, which our children may find out about someday. Will my son somehow be able to know that I ate sushi and had some beers before realizing that I was pregnant, that I was on the verge of thinking my body wasn't able to bear fruit?

But maybe it's comforting to be able to speak from beyond the grave, to let people know your truth, that, yes, your body was bested, but it wasn't your heart. Your heart was strong stuff.

Angelyn DeBord

Poems Of Ancient Grannies

Oh, ancient grannies
where are your poems?
Not written on the hallowed page beside
those of
Milton or Blake
Shelly or Byron
I do not find them written there.

Not penned down,
your words are lifted up,
written in the air,
clear before my searching eyes

And even to my ear
the cadence of your poems is heard
in the rhythm
of the clear eyed man.
He's been mothered well, I think.
I see his mother's poetry
written above his clear bright eyes,
words sketched with a tender hand
across that smooth forehead.

Ancient grannies.
I know your words were sweet and strong
when I see your grandbabies
tilt their ear
at a whimsical phrase or a lilting song.

Where are your poems? In my blood,
in the images of my dreams,
in the cycles of my life.
Words strong with pictures
of what was and is and will be,
written not on the hallowed page,
but written in my veins,
written secretly there with your blood.

Mimi Railey Merritt

Mercy

She thought I wasn't listening,
my grandmother chatting with antique aunties
about wrinkle creams and laxatives.
But busy dressing Barbie dolls in the parlor's far corner,
I heard her remember falling down church steps at 15.
An uncushioned pew still hurt her tailbone, she said.

She seldom took her prayers to church.
Preachers preached love sometimes but mostly fear
while she brewed sassafras roots into tea for sick friends
and served cornbread and fried chicken
to hobos my mother remembered long ago knocking at the back door.

Church pews were for funerals,
for her first born, laid to rest at 46
from a blood clot bursting in his brain;
for her baby sister, 17 years her junior,
a once round-faced toddler who grew up frail
and worn out from pain and the pills that killed it.

The Sunday morning excuses were many.
Still in her slip when church bells rang,
uncertain where she had hung her best dress,
dentures kept in a bedside waterglass were missing,
a dizzy headache needed a BC powder in ginger ale,
an uneasy stomach a soda cracker.

The church would be cold, and the newspaper tempted,
the beautiful First Lady smiling on the front page,
a young mother who soon would be photographed
in a blood-smattered pink suit
and days later in black, face veiled beside her little boy
saluting his father's casket.

My grandmother did not like church pews.
I saw her kneeling by her bed at night, though,
gray hair hanging long down her back,
hair that by day she swept into a knot at neck's nape,
wisps escaping as she fried flounder and beat biscuits

in her small kitchen's damp heat.
I saw her on her knees, ghostlike by her bed,
and when I crept closer in the dark,
I heard her asking for her daily bread,
and my grandmother, pained by wooden seats,
confessed trespasses on knees pressed hard against wooden floorboards.

One Sunday before church we found her in her garden,
tending roses, knees in dirt,
hem of her blue silk dress trailing loamy soil,
her black patent leather purse reflecting sun,
as though she had been on her way
to join us.

Maybe she had walked down back steps,
the church a short walk in a town of many steeples,
when her eyes, blue as her dress and farsighted with age,
spotted the Peace rose, its yellow and pink petals
catching sun while framing a deeper coral center.

Maybe she had walked toward it to smell a fragrance
sweeter than the Chanel
she often dabbed at her wrist,
remembering my grandfather giving her
the bottled scent of rose and jasmine.

Maybe it was his last smile
or the rosebud often pinned to his shirt pocket
that she saw as she dropped to her knees
to pull close the Peace bloom,
face arched to the rising sun.

Kate Dieringer

Surgical Sexism

chainsaw (noun): medical tool first designed for use in obstetrics, termed
osteotome, from the Greek osteo (bone) tomi (cut), translation; bone cutter

textbook omits mention of prototype designed
      to cleave calcium of body's strongest architecture
      a thing that grants power to shatter wishbone's grasp

note the mewling red cavern, after she is opened, the root cracked clean
the newborn's gummed grin marks an unkind sign of scalpel's success
a mottled limb leering out towards the butcher
waiting

consider this lesson from botany's discipline
shear hibiscus back and the center will riot back plush, full of red
clutch of fisted petal from wood
against tool's metallic flourish

consider the flesh of your own hand

consider the body juicy heart full of fury
two fists held up to a buzz of teeth
on an endless chain

consider this note, stuffed deep in the dust of your pocket
blood ringing your wrists, stains on the coat's white sleeves

      keep this next to your darkest ink pens
      closest to your sharpest keys

Diana Hays

Flood

bare mountains black behind
the deluge
stripmined watershed
no hindrance to muddy waters

trees, mattresses, used tires
course through
Hazard, Harlan, Blackey
Jeremiah, Kingdom Come
Pampers in the trees just
another sad verse in the
Kentucky song

Kingdom Come. Please.
Kingdom Come.
turn these waters into wine
freeze them into stained glass

behind us our heroes
and our dead
will live forever in
red, cobalt, emerald
windows
and memory

we will gather round a
bonfire of broken trees
raise our eyes
and sing

Amy McCleese Nichols

Still Frozen

the ground lies fresh, controlled and tight
beneath layers of worthless watered diamond shine.
there is no motion here, no flex when walking feet
chink and crunch across mint-candy grass, no
give when lungs inhale sharp air, closing up at
the bite—no cover for the bare arms of the oak
standing, a great twisted obelisk of remembrance.
it all waits, breathless, for an ancient signal
that will peal out in storm and flood, washing free
the insects and seeds to love and loosen, unfurling
in the all-glory of early spring.

Amy McCleese Nichols

Teenagers Going to Town

There is no need to talk, really.
Instead, we sing, faces lit with nothing but starlight,
Headlights of others flicking past as we pass by.
Our ostensible errand eggs,
Our real aim the tug of the curvy road,
Lit edges fading into the long grass, the hillside,
The eyes of the occasional animal wandering by.
If we are lucky enough to have time for the long way home
(The backroad, by the Amish house),
Perhaps you will turn off the headlights
And we will see the road again in moonlight,
All silvered this time, and the hills and houses lit up just beyond.

Celia Lawren

When Edgar Meyer Plays Double Bass

He bows the strings slowly, closes his eyes
To cold Appalachian melancholy.
Embracing the neck & shoulders,
He pulls the upright closer, swings
As he works up & down the bouts,
Grazing the strings, pulling off
To pluck another, like lovers
In a back room, each stroke of their bodies
Plays a song of consolation for the lonely
Next door in the bar, twirling
Paper umbrellas in their icy elixirs.
Meyers fingers just above the bridge,
And high notes in stilettos, tails straight up,
Strut through dark alleys.
Then he drops low, strings moan,
Conjuring prodigal homecomings,
Like my ex, the morning after,
Pouring vodka down the drain,
Vowing *never again*,
Again & again.

Frauke Palmer
Dream Catcher

Lisa Parker

You Can't Leave It When You Go

> *I cursed this place when I was young*
> *for cursing me with a broken tongue*
> *and hiding the horizon from my view.*
> *These days I can't quit thinking of*
> *the land whose shoulders blocked the sun*
> *and people who speak music like I do.*
> *— Tiffany Williams*

My mother's practiced tongue never gave away
the hollers, the one-room schoolhouse at the mouth
of Garden Creek, never gave away the spring house
cut in the hillside or its flat sod roof she could walk out on
from straight off the road.

When Granddaddy moved them to flat land, valley down
where his boys would find steel or wood and not
the Black Lung trap of Red Jacket and Oakwood Smokeless,
she learned ridicule quickly, tucked accent and dialect
quietly behind teeth and tongue, made herself *bookish*.
She chose paralegal over lumber secretary, put back funds,
took in her baby sister, put in a phone at her folks' house,
married an Army Yankee, taught her children
mountain harmonies, gospel sung in the car with her sister
Ruth the perfect vocal fit, two pitch pieces puzzled together
every Saturday as we drove neighborhoods,
yardsale after yardsale, piling clothes and dishes
between children, between chorus canons
of *Some Wondrous Day*,
When the roll is called up yonder.

Downhome was said with sweet nostalgia,
with stories of Bea and Het who made her fried apple pies,
taught her to string leather breeches beans, never knotted
her toddler thread so she could *sew* at the great quilting frame.
My mother's practiced tongue never gave away
downhome in its totality, the little girl's belly
never quite full, payphone calls on Saturday mornings
to local jails, a child seeking answers
for her mother, a familiar drunkard's AWOL,

a *tracking down* that left her a lifelong hatred of phones,
a fear of absence.

Downhome was the constant background song we could hum
but never bring to full voice or lyric, things
she relegated to the margins, things
she couldn't fully push back: tears at the smell
of oranges, those rare sweet treats, or peppermint balls
that melted in our mouths and made her turn her head away,
warnings not to get in the car with Uncle Walter,
sweet as he was, or go to the woods
where our great-grandpa's still and burnt-frame house
stood long after he was gone from them.

Downhome was stripped of something,
of hard truths, of mountaintops long gone,
pineful stories of bootlegging and *back in the day*,
but also, sweet Jesus, also filling the stripped places
back in with younguns in that valley, piled
14-deep on stairs to sing Christmas songs
before gift-opening, to learn callouses
on tight mandolin strings, harmonies on Carter classics,
or stories of grandfathers who walked across states and mountains
to build stone walls along the Blue Ridge Parkway with the CCC,
and grandmothers who painted walnut shells and glued
pine needles and crimson leaves to wood pieces to sell
as *folk art* for shoe money, to teach herbal medicine,
dousing, mourning dove calls, and the shrill magic
of a grass blade pulled tight between thumbs,
against lips, blown into song, all the things
we wouldn't learn in classrooms they insisted on, all the things
that would follow us as they follow my mother, the salty
sweet citrus-sting of those hills and hollers,
all the meanings of the words *broken* and *blessed* and *kin*.

Lisa Parker

Cannery In Seasons
for my cousins

Summer

Hide and seek, a perfect asylum,
place to cool a sweaty body
on damp concrete floor, tuck back
between musty, bent-boarded
shelves of white half-runner beans, peach
halves, chow-chow jars that slosh cardinal
red and lush green, pluck a small jar
of bread and butters to press chilled glass
against cheek and forehead, watch the door
through liquid shift of celery seed, clove,
and crisp cucumber, everything sealed,
sheltered.

Fall

Run fingers over squat jars
their bellies a raised glass lattice
that glows amber in sunshaft,
sulphured sorghum that shifts
a lazy wave when tilted, jars
of pear and apple butter,
burnt siennas and cinnamon speckled,
golden orange butternut squash, pumpkin
and carrot toward shelf-back, straw baskets
filled with sturdy gourds and Indian corn.
Move straight-back chair from yard, sit
between cedar barrels to string shucky beans,
door open to watch leaf-fall, listen
for Winter in the branch-clatter of pin oak
and winged elms.

Winter

Heavy enough for their own shelf,
generous jars of venison, pork, and tenderloin rest
in their own fat, what they would call

confit in a good restaurant.
Pull jars of pale pearl onions and pickled beets,
choose from row after row of pinto beans,
sweet relish, sacks of meal and flour
from covered barrels—
hunkering food.
These are the meals of fireplace-sitting,
of clock-tick evenings when cold presses to bone
and stillness calls for thick breads and bowls
of steaming soup and stews heavy with game.
Touch these shelves with reverent hands.
These shelves house jars of *you will make it,*
there is enough, and *next year we will put back more.*

Spring

Cherrywood-smoked catfish and jars
of rainbow trout for March, a signal
to Winter that we're pulling out of her
sleepy reach, toward all the ice breaks
and snow melt, the drying out and fresh bud,
last killing frost, and all the signs we will plant by.
Collect rocket and dewberries before deer and birds.
First jars filled are greens and cabbage, eggs peeled
and placed in beet-purple brine.
Open window.
Pull chair from between cedar barrels,
sit in doorway.
Pay attention.
Fire-throated warblers call down from hemlocks,
a skink warms itself on mountain rock, tiny squirrels
chase each other, a cacophony of dried leaves underfoot.
Pollinators move on daffodils and tulips at the cannery's edge
and a long-beaked flicker snatches grubs beneath him.
Mind all the birdcall and budding that map your path
and plan for soil beneath you, all the things you will grow
and pluck, boil down and can to fill jars on the shelves behind you,
empty now but for pink blossom reflections
of arbutus and chartreuse hickories.

Catherine Carter

This house

The year's sauerkraut is coldly cooking itself
down in the cellar of the house of this life,
whose concrete floor holds the bodies down.

Upstairs, dogs are fighting
or play-fighting on the skin rug near the stove
where birch-twigs turn back to their native flame,
and a man is kneading bread like living flesh.

Some of the children are playing Balderdash
while the rest watch TV, all
but the two who are tormenting a third
into pitching herself down the stairs:
another emergency call.

This house has sealed rooms,
more than I'll ever see.
Some are full of stones; at the turn
of the weather, smell the chill of their breath.
Listen: the cry of a door's secret hinge.

Outside, there are more windows than inside,
flashing sunrise before fading
into siding as the bright day swells.

The whitefoot mice know; when they slip out
of the walls into the rooms we see,
we find them next day on the rug
in a soil of blood: the cats also know.

Some rooms are roofed with limbs
interlaced, floored with a rubble
of roots. Some rooms are packed tight
with rotting shirts, spoiled meat.

That whisper of water isn't the pipes
but the creek that runs under the floor.

The attic's flying squirrels give birth to kits.
There's a dead bumblebee on the sill.
Sunchokes ripen toward December,
the roasting, the eating.

The washing is never done, the mail
heaps up, the children
keep torturing each other
as soon as you turn away.
You're behind from the day you sign the lease.

In the eaves, the wren sings all year.
Under the foundation, the dead do, too.

Nothing is ever finished, nothing
ever simple, the number
of rooms will never be known,
not here, not in this house.

Catherine Carter

Spring tonic

Every year there's watercress in the runoff
ditch, froth of foam-bloom in the culvert that drains
a highway a parking lot a construction
site a few gratuitous cow
fields, meaning there's not enough iodine
in the world, that cress will never be safe
to eat. So with field-mustard creasies
not up yet, you turn for your equinox green
back to muddy yards, cracks in foundations
of buildings, hairy bittercress:
its tiny pepper-spice, its blunt scallop-curl
leaves, its satyr-labor to spread its glitter
of cruciform flowers over gardens waste
places intramural fields by detonating slender
siliques in a micro-ballista sputter
of seed. Chopped into salad, sipped
over soup, gnawed in the raw, it's what you need
now: deep vivid bite of what
comes first, blazes its way, takes
cold rain-slits into its own
flesh, takes the first and only chance
it has. Spring tonic that wrings
mouth and bowels because still fresh
from the dark cauldron's boil and spit;
taste of renewal strong enough, in its spiral
basal-rosette heart, for this very world:
its sudsy ditches greasy roads whirling weed
eaters grinding clocks night sticks raised
to strike. Taste of resistance photo-
synthesized into unfettered
exuberance. Attar of bitter.

Valerie Nieman

Note left for the woman buying this house

You might want to know
that after three barren years, the purple irises
bloomed this spring, just before their useless
toes might have been yanked from the earth.
One neighbor has cats.
The other, kids.
The bushes along the fence are blueberries,
but you won't get a one unless you net them.
Birds are clever and relentless.
The patio door has been replaced. Twice.
Day lilies will trumpet your arrival,
but wild ginger will conceal itself, as is its nature.
The dog-tooth violets will be gone.
Be careful:
The ramp to the shed is treacherous after rain.
Some things will be imponderable.
Doors on two of the bedrooms won't latch.
(The casings are cracked where they were wrenched open.)
Spider lilies will surprise you, coming out of nowhere.
The walls have been painted beige,
sealing in the cries and curses.
The carpet is new.
Wait to dig. Buried lines and conduits cross the yard.
Some things won't have risen, yet.

Patsy Kisner

The Farm

Something's always
needing feeding—
beaks and snouts,
muzzles with sturdy molars
used for grinding grain.

Some days I feel
like I'm breaking
off pieces of my
own self, giving
too much of me away.

At dark
I open books,
read the cravings
my loves have
sent to me
on paper. I study
the lines,
the perfect diction,
the turn of a word
in ways I
could not think.
I read until
I'm full, then
add ink
to my own pages.

In the morning
I'll start
over, filling all
those mouths
with one type
of seed
or another.

Diane Tarantini

The Best Part Is Jumping In

Today's gonna be a scorcher. Wanna go swimming? I know the perfect place. The water's so beautiful, a deep, saturated teal. Like blue raspberry and lime Slush Puppies mixed together. Or a fancy cocktail made of Midori and Blue Curacao.

The water temperature's always just right. Not so cold your heart stops when you dive in, but not like bathwater either.

The best part is jumping in, but first you have to climb the rocky, dry path. Be careful to watch out for the pull tabs. They'll slice your foot right open. Make you bleed like crazy. To be safe, take turns looking where you're going and glancing down. A tetanus shot might be a good idea too. In case you get cut. Or bit.

Oh, gosh, wait! You don't even know how to get there.

First you have to cross the bridge from West Virginia to Ohio and turn right. Then you need to watch for the old Esso station on the left. After that, be on the lookout for the wild boys' place, also on the left. With its faded red barn and split rail fence, the property resembles a farm.

The wild boys who live there are nuts. Cute too. In that I'm-bad-and-I-might-just-convince-you-to-be-bad-too kind of way. They live life more outdoors than in. Up at the swimming hole. Camping out in the woods. Down at the river, fishing.

The one time they took us in their barn, I saw the scariest thing ever. Saddest too. They kept a pit bull in there. Back before the breed was cool. Back before Michael Vick got caught in his vice. They couldn't let the dog outside because he was crazy vicious. He'd kill anything with four legs. It was the guys' fault. They turned the dog that way—probably to make him fight. So he'd hate all animals, using a rag, they'd pick up something dead then spend a good 20 minutes smacking the dog in the face with it. They started small and worked their way up. Squirrels to possums to groundhogs.

According to the boys, one time the dog escaped the barn and killed a neighbor's goat. I kid you not. After that, they made him wear one of those super mean collars with big spikes that dug into his neck if he made a wrong move. *And* they chained him to a post in the barn.

I never understood why the dog hated other animals. Why didn't he hate the boys? Heck, why didn't we?

It was the wild boys who showed us the swimming hole. Well, one of them.

Shortly after we passed the Esso station, that's when we spotted the guys. Sitting at a picnic table out in their front yard, beneath the shade of a sprawling maple tree, throwing back PBRs.

After Suzy coasted her Subaru wagon into their driveway, we sent Laura Jane over to ask for directions. Boys'll tell her anything. Especially when she's wearing her teeny weenie white bikini and blue jean short shorts. Suze and I rolled down our car windows so we could catch the directions to the swimming hole.

Laura Jane ducked between the top and middle split rail, and as she sashayed over to the boys, the biggest one snickered. "Well, well, well. What have we here? I seen that same sorta swing on a back porch once." From the car, we witnessed Laura flashing her brilliant Ultra-Brite smile and flipping her almost black, bra strap-length hair behind her golden shoulder.

"How you guys doing? My friends and I'd like to check out the secret swimming hole that's supposed to be around here. You all know where it's at?"

"You mean the filled-up strip mine?" the youngest one said. He was good-looking. Kind of reminded me of John Denver, only smaller. Suze and I watched as the bigger boys' eyes went all squinty and their hands closed into fists.

"Them's pissed," Suzy whispered.

Ignoring his friends, Little John Denver grinned up at Laura Jane— she's close to six feet tall—then pointed toward the woods.

"See that rusted oil drum? When you all get to it, keep your eyes peeled because the turn up the mountain's right beyond that."

The biggest boy shoved Little John. "Ah, man! Why'd you do that? We don't want no girls up there."

"Says who?" Little John said. He turned back to Laura. "I can take you all up, if you want."

John Denver's name was actually Danny.

"Why's it called the strip mine?" I said from the back seat. He twisted to face me.

"'Cause that's what it used to be. When there was no more coal, they flooded it. Wait till you see it. The water's the coolest color ever."

After Suzy parked the car, Danny led us up the steep, crunchy peanut butter path. Along the way, he held back brambly branches so we wouldn't scratch our sleek, shaved that morning legs.

All of a sudden, the trail ended at the edge of a sandstone cliff, twenty or more feet over the opaque and aqua water.

As soon as I asked, "How do you get down there?" I slapped my hands over my ears because I didn't want to know the answer. I hate heights.

Danny snorted. "You jump, silly."

He stepped toward me, I blinked, and before I knew it, I was hurtling through the dry July air. Next to Danny. Over and over I backstroked my arms. Trying to . . . I don't know. Save myself? Make it back to the cliff's edge?

When I hit the water, my eyes and mouth slammed shut. My hair felt like silky seaweed as it brushed my arms. I opened my eyes and through the turquoise murk I saw the sun beaming above me. I shoved down handfuls of water to get up. To the light. To the air.

Once there, I dog-paddled, whipping my head left and right in an effort to locate my gal pals. They waved from way up there. I cupped my hand and twirled it again and again.

"Jump in! The water's awesome!"

Twenty feet away Danny floated on his back, smiling up at the clean slate of a sky. I stretched out and did the same. Filled my lungs with little puffs of air so I could stay on top of the water.

After a while, Danny used his right foot to point out the path that led back up to the top. "As good as this water feels," he said, "the best part is jumping in."

Lisa Kamolnick

Samba
for Bruce

I can hear Rio from 4,833 miles away
clear to Tennessee's upper right corner.
She sashays in
on a Latinate wind.
A boughed *bateria* beats an invitation
in synchronized syncopation—dance with me.
Trees sway,
lay an undeniably recognizable rhythm
born in West Africa, rooted in Brazil,
blown to God's country.

Wind's aspirate hisses
slither along oaks tip to root
as trails of butterflies float ever higher
in filigree flutter.
Shrill songbird trills and cheeps repeat.
Geese gaggle in a brassy airborne parade,
lay down their sensual moans in the music.
Can you feel it?

A Brazilian invocation blows across Appalachia—
Rio rubs Rocky Top's stubbled winter ridges,
lays hands on a hollow's shapely form.
Hips tilted, gyrating, Brazil
rolls through fertile fields
to my homestead on a snow-dusted hill.
An *apito's* infectious inflection settles in—
moves me, prays me.
Will music save me?
                    Is God
                    on the way?
Maybe I'll find Him
come Ash Wednesday.

"I want you to know you are beautiful, that you have the entire world in the palm of your hands, and it's a gorgeous thing having time.
— Megan Krzmarzick (1985–2000)

Julie Elman
You are beautiful

154

Pamela Hirschler

Transmutation

If I somehow find silence
for a moment, I am on the water.
The wake angles in, the slap,
the scrape, the boat at the dock,
a swirl of blood in the hold,
all that's left from the catch,
weathered planks, splintery
gray, a trickle of water
over the edge like grief.

Pamela Hirschler

All things Want to Fly

All things want to fly,
the bees in the lavender,
returned after an absence,

the girl on the pink bike,
her hair streaming behind her,
me at the window, watching

the neighbor's dog as he limps
to the curb, even the unseen,
the humpback whale, breaching

against the sky.

Angela O'Curran-Lopez

Poverty Knob

growing up
i never really knew
that we were poor.

you see
when you are
three
a single wide trailer
looks like a
mansion

everyone had
a bulldozer
in their driveway
and a couple
broke down cars
parked out back
by the old chicken coop

right?

i mean
at least one was a
lincoln
a 1978 continental

rumor has it
somewhere near the
fishing pond
my dad built a
cold war
fallout shelter
underground

we had a
beautiful garden
and a deep freeze
full of
deer meat

that we were given
in exchange for
letting people hunt on our
land

corn and peas
and lumpy mashed potatoes
were great for sunday dinner
but the real winner
for a five year old
were those bologna
sandwiches
on soft white bread
and store brand
spaghetti-os
from the aluminum
can

i don't remember
ever having
name brand
snacks
in the kitchen
but my mom
always seemed to have
her winston 100s
longs not shorts
everywhere
she went

my dad affectionately
called the place
where he hung the cars
he was fixing
by a giant hook
and chain
hanging from a
hundred-year-old
tree
and the two room
"house"
with no indoor
plumbing

where he cut out
the wall
and attached
the trailer
through a "hallway"
he created himself
and six acres of
property
that he owned free and clear
"good old poverty knob"

from the time that
i was born
until i turned
eight years old
when my father
died
i just called it
home.

Chrissie Anderson Peters

The Most Wonderful Time of the Year

Seeing as how I lived only 90 minutes away, I had to go home for Christmas every year. Which was typically on Christmas Eve because Jared, my husband (whom I had imported from Chicago), was an RN and usually ended up working Christmas Day. This was actually fine, though, as it kept with our tradition of opening gifts on Christmas Eve.

This particular year, the weather was clear, but bitterly cold. I had hoped for snow, but none had fallen at home. Typically colder where my family lived, I still held out hope. Alas, we arrived to cold-blowing wind, but not a single snowflake in sight. We got out of the SUV, our food in hand, and started into Grandma and Grandpa's house. There was a full-size plastic nativity scene outside in the yard, just beside the porch, but something was different. "Jared, is it me, or do all of the nativity figures have ropes around them?"

Jared, remaining absolutely deadpan, said, "Yep, right down to the Baby Jesus."

I went inside, while Jared took a smoke break before entering. I was met with loud greetings, hugs, people happily taking our food to the kitchen, asking where Jared was (when everyone knew the answer), asking how we had been. . . .

But I mostly ignored all of that and walked up to my grandmother, a look of concern on my face. "Grandma, why are there ropes around your nativity scene figures?"

"Oh, Daphne! We had some awful winds this week and they just about blew away!"

"Did you think about trying to maybe anchor them to the ground? Something other than baler twine around their necks tied to the stable?"

"Oh, your Uncle Bob said this would be easier. [Uncle Bob being the one who did all the handy work around the house and farm, of course.] It doesn't show from the road." Which was true, I guess, but it sure as shooting showed if you pulled into the driveway.

Grandpa piped up from his chair in the corner, "Daphne, I told her that it looked downright blasphemous!"

I excused myself and joined Jared back out on the front porch. "They almost blew away in the wind," I informed him, regarding the nativity figures. "It still seems awfully cruel to have them tied up like that."

"Cruel? They get to stay *out here*, and we have to be *in there* for the next few hours," he looked sideways at the front door.

"Jared! That's not nice!" I scolded.

We went inside, together this time, and all the commotion ensued again, this time for Jared's benefit, as though he hadn't heard it the first time around. A man of few words, Jared said his hellos, then took a seat opposite Grandpa's chair in the living room, shouting back and forth with him for a couple of minutes before both men tired of pretending to be interested in the art of conversation among all the other noise around them.

Grandma had to show off all her Christmas cards to me. She always hung every Christmas card that she received in the doorways. She had done this for as long as I could remember. It was an act of pride, a contest of sorts, to see how many she would receive each year, from how far they would come. By the time she got to be in her 70's, lots of people sent her Christmas cards. I opened a few to see who had sent them. I recognized most as church friends and family. A few were unfamiliar, so I asked. "Who's Agnes?"

She walked over to look at it. "Andy!" She called to my grandpa. "Is Agnes your half-sister's daughter-in-law's cousin?"

Grandpa shrugged his shoulders, "I don't know, Deborah, maybe."

My mom chimed in, "I thought it was Dad's sister's husband's niece?"

We went through four or five more like that. Jared tried hard not to laugh, as he caught my attention and shook his finger indicating that I should leave her alone and just let her be proud of her cards.

I turned to the Christmas tree, which actually looked spectacular, and told Grandma that it looked really nice. There was new tinsel, new LED lights, several new ornaments, but also many of my old favorite, cherished ornaments from childhood. It really looked just about perfect! "Your Aunt Sandy and your mom decorated that for me on Thanksgiving. You wouldn't know that, though, because you were in Chicago with Jared's family!" *Ah, there we go, the guilt trip.*

Jared came over to admire it with me and put his arm around me, as though to protect me from the rest of the barbs that would surely fly about us visiting his family once a year. Being the tall man that he was, though, he reached over to lean the angel back, as it looked like she was leaning forward. That's when it happened.

Her hair came off! He didn't realize that it was just kinda taped on there with Scotch tape and it came right off when he accidentally touched it. Grandma screamed that he'd torn up her "antique" angel, and everyone came rushing into the living room to try to fix things back, so Grandma would calm down and not have a holiday heart attack, which she was prone to do sometimes.

Poor Jared just stood there open-mouthed. I pulled him over to the piano bench. "It's okay, honey. She's had that angel since the first Christmas I can remember," I laughed. "You didn't know that she was wearing the equivalent of a Dolly Parton wig!"

Things started to settle down a bit from there, even if they didn't necessarily quiet down, and finally Grandpa yelled out above the deafening din, "Is it time to eat yet, or not?"

Jared quickly jumped to his feet. "Grandpa, I think that's a good idea. I'll go get the turkey out of the oven. Do you want to carve it?"

Grandpa waved his hand and said quietly under the roar from the other side of the room, "It'll just fall off the bone, anyway, so you go on, Jared. I'm getting too old to hold that electric knife too steady, anyway," he winked at me.

My Aunt Sandy, the baby of the family, and only twelve years older than I was, had escaped to the kitchen to remove her trademark homemade rolls from the oven, as I was working on pulling desserts out of the fridge and coolers.

Uncle Cory turned thanks and Jared started carving the bird with the same expression of horror his eyes always held when it came to Grandma's turkey. As a teenager, we bought pizza for me the day before because I hated turkey. It turned out that I didn't hate turkey, per se, just *Grandma's* turkey. It was the driest, nastiest stuff I'd ever tasted. It was like chewing paper! As an adult, she started buying a ham, especially for me, as if the pizza were an abomination at the holiday table. No one else complained. I guess they had never had anything different, so they didn't know any better. As for me, I'd had Jared's Thanksgiving turkey cooked on a Weber grill and it was most succulent bird in the universe! I watched Jared finish off the remaining damage to the turkey carcass, my Aunt Pam grabbing a drumstick, and reached for a couple of pieces of ham to go with my myriad of sides.

After lunch, Grandpa kicked back in his recliner and was snoring away, sleeping with his tongue hanging out of his mouth, a la Michael Jordan. Uncle Bob had gone home as soon as he ate, not being overly social. My stepfather, and sister, too, had gone home, and would pick up my mother later. Uncle Cory had either gone up on the hilltop to hunt or commune with God, depending on the temperatures. Jared was flipping through channels, not really looking for anything in particular. That left all of us women to find something to do. And it was always the same thing. Rummy.

Rummy was something of a family tradition among the women. There was only one problem. Grandma cheated. Everyone let her by with it. Except me. I was just too competitive to have her win by laying down all of her cards after her turn had passed and someone had "gone out," because, she "forgot to lay them down" on her last turn. Especially when this happened nearly every hand. I politely called her out on it a few times, and she refused to pay me any mind. When it finally came down to me beating her, beating my mother, or losing, I finally told her no. "No, Grandma! You *cannot* lay down those cards! It's not your turn, anymore.

If Mom beats me this game, she will beat me honestly, but I'm not sitting here and having you *cheat* me out of a win!"

Well, I had said the magic word. *"Cheat?!?* You think I'm *cheating???* I'm just a poor, helpless old woman and I can't help that I forget..."

And thus began a litany of wrongs I had committed against her during rummy games for years, being mean and cruel, when none of her other grandchildren would have dared to do or say such awful things to her. Her other grandchildren loved her, she declared. "Yes, I noticed that none of them sent Christmas cards or called," I said aloud, thinking initially that I'd only said it inside my head.

Her gasp was more than audible. It was damned near palpable, as she clutched her heart, and exclaimed, "Well, I *never!*"

Jared, overhearing the ruckus from the living room, called out, asking if it was about time to head home so he could get some rest before he had to get up and be at work at 5:00 a.m. the next morning.

"No," Grandma insisted, "you keep playing. Since *I'm* the cheater, I'll just go put things away."

Well, that was the end of rummy. Everyone went to put things away, even though everything had been put away before rummy ever started. I got my casserole dish and went to wake up Grandpa to give him a hug.

"I guess *cheaters* don't get hugs," Grandma exclaimed with a huff.

"Yes, *you* get a hug," I answered, exasperated. "I was getting Grandpa first, so I can come over to the door and put my shoes on after I hug you, and not have to walk all the way back across the living room. I know that I'm not allowed to track up your floors, walking through with my shoes on."

I'd lost track of the number of guilt trips this was, but I sure wished that I was racking up some sort of frequent flyer miles for them all!

Grandma went to the kitchen and got her purse. "Here, now, Daphne, you and Jared take your Christmas checks."

"Grandma, it really isn't necessary," I started.

"I sent one to all the grandkids," she informed me, making me feel oh-so-very special. "Remember, now, they're postdated, so don't try to cash them until after the third of the month. You have a Merry Christmas!"

I took a deep breath, hugged her neck, and kissed her cheek. Defeated, I muttered, "You have a Merry Christmas, too, Grandma."

Then everyone started calling out Merry Christmas, like it had been a perfect day. And, maybe in our own little bizarre world, it had come pretty close, I thought, realizing that I was probably about as weird and had almost as many idiosyncrasies and neuroses as the rest of them, just in different ways.

As we walked down the sidewalk towards the car, I looked over at the nativity scene, now lit up in the dark of the evening. "Poor Baby Jesus," I lamented, shaking my head.

"Lucky Wise Men," Jared insisted.

Lacy Snapp

Lore

Green and blue grain, purple that borderlines on black
stretches out beneath my hands as I pull lumber
out of the back of my dad's truck. *It's called rainbow
poplar,* he says in a voice that to me feels ancient
and all-knowing, like he's letting me in on a secret
available only to a select few. *Next to a mountain stream
that tree grew, pulling, pulling in nutrients from
a source deep within the earth.* As I gaze deep within
its rings, I can see myself. A Gemini-moon mix of different
personalities. I, too, have pulled from the world
around me. Purple patches from traveling, experiences
that forever changed a young Johnson City girl. Blue
waves of insecurities forged once the universe became
bigger—black streaks of bad habits picked up from people
who I now realize were just as lost as me. Greenness
that tries to hold on to the person I once was. As we stack
the wood inside the shop, I find each board is drastically
different—a cosmic affirmation that I will also continue
to change, evolve as I pull, pull from what's around me.
To this day, I don't know if my dad's legend is even true,
and I haven't the heart to find out, research if he is wrong.
I prefer to be the barefoot young woman, ankle deep
in the creek, absorbing what's around me, wondering
what future story a two-inch slice of my soul will tell.

Lacy Snapp

Daily Routine—An Ars Poetica

During the summers, I start pulling forgotten lumber
    from storage units every morning by eight a.m.
        The current stack—a mound of beech bowed from years
            of neglect. *It's shit wood anyways*, my dad says,
                splinters and cracks no matter how
                    carefully it's handled.
Twelve feet above my head, I try to figure how
    I will manage to get it down—climb on the lower rows,
        pray they hold my weight, where random boards protrude
        like harpoons lost in Moby Dick's side.

While I ascend, simple phrases catch in my ears
    as spider webs do in my hair and branch out—spread,
        link together as I take little pieces from radio commercials
            or mainstream song lyrics that I wish I didn't know
            the words to. The first half
of the workday is a time for repeating: Step up. Balance.
    Pull the highest board out. Let it tip to the ground.
        Step off. Pick up. Carry to its new home. Double check
        that its aligned. Return to the stack—As my body shifts

into automation, my mind tests its ability to withstand
    the pressure of memory. A poem begins as the morning dew
        evaporates, starts with an image gathered
            unexpectedly: the perfectly preserved mouse carcass
            in a gap between two rows. Silverfish slipping
into their own reclaimed utopias. Carpenter bees flirting
    with overhead beams—while they tunnel, sawdust falls,
        sticking to the cobwebs I already wear, pairing together
        borrowed lyrics with beings that merely needed a voice.

Repeat until lunchtime, stomach growling and stanza
    about to burst from my mouth, I scavenge for a discarded
        block in the scrap box, settle for a two-by-four wedge.
            The poem pours out as my sandwich goes in, taking
            time between each bite to tap the cadence
            on my work bench stool.
For all the hours past noon, the stacking-lumber-process resumes while
    my brain takes time to decompress. Pencil and cubed poem
        in my pocket, I wait for the final words to find me—
            unmistakable as a newly forged splinter beneath
            the skin.

Diana Ferguson
Coffee Time

167

Tamara M. Baxter

Killing Oranges

I read in a murder mystery magazine at the back of Ziggy's Newsstand that I can kill my husband by driving a nail in his ear while he is asleep, then, pull it out. No one will find out. The ear does not bleed, so there is no evidence. No blood. That is important to me, because I hate the sight of blood.

An icicle will work as well as a nail. The evidence melts into a puddle and evaporates. Tricky, though, because icicles are unpredictable. The icicle could melt in my sweaty hand if I hesitate too long. Too long before winter. There are long, sharp icicles frozen to the guttering during January.

I can kill him through his eyeball, too. Pull back the lid and drive a wire through the corner of the eye, through the open socket, carefully, carefully, into the soft tissue of the brain. Make sure it is a fine, strong wire. Long and thin.

Mother's pearl hatpin?

Make sure I have steady hands, determination, and concentration. Make sure he is doped into a deep sleep so he will lie still, cooperate. Be warned about the blood. A drop or two at least, the magazine says

I am sure now that I must kill him with a nail. I am used to nails. Daddy was a carpenter. He built houses and banks, and buildings for companies. Daddy drank, too, and hammered nails. I am used to the pound, pound, pounding of nails in planks.

I am used to the smell of liquor, rough beard like sandpaper on my face, eyes swimming through hazy puddles above me. But never the blood in beads along the floor where I run to find Mother.

Mother? Mother? Mother?

Daddy would not build for Mother, even if the doors fell from their hinges. Stubborn.

I consider buying a gun, but there will be evidence. Papers to sign, the gun salesman, squint-eyed, attentive, a sponge soaking up every characteristic of my face, remembering my nervous twitching, my silly questions, my excuses. With a gun, there will be blood.

The body? Getting rid of it, and the gun? Too much mess. Too risky. Too nerve-racking.

Perhaps I will manage the gun? I will wait until he is asleep, put a pillow over his head, point, pull the trigger? I will be scared. He will not drink enough of the liquor I have laced with sleeping medicine. I am standing over him. I will close my eyes a second to gather courage, and he will wake up, suddenly, grab the gun from my sweaty hands. Shoot me.

My blood all over the floor and the walls. All over Daddy. He will tell them he killed me in self-defense. They will believe Daddy.

No, I am smarter than Mother. Much smarter.

I find *EAR* in the encyclopedia and with my husband's carpenter's pencil, I draw twenty-two ears along a two-by-four from a pile of lumber he is saving. I practice hammering nails into the wooden ears late in the afternoons at the back of the garage. I use my husband's workbench, his nails, his hammer. He is a carpenter. He builds houses.

The girls are playing outdoors in their little rubber swimming pool. I hear them giggling between the pounds of my hammer. Their giggling distracts me, and I hit my thumb.

There is blood on the plank. Drops of my blood on the white plank.

"What are you doing, Mommy? Why are you hammering nails?" They have found me at the back of the garage sucking the hurt from my thumb.

"I am building a new doghouse for Trixie," I tell them, tasting salt. They believe me.

"Can we hammer, too?" They giggle, pulling a ball-peen hammer from their daddy's toolbox.

"NO! NO! NO!" I shout at them. "You must *NEVER, NEVER, NEVER* hammer nails!"

They cover their ears, look at me. They run away to the pool. I do not understand their eyes, why my little girls look at me that way when I am trying so hard. They do not understand that I have seen him. He does not know I watch. But I have seen him patting their ruffled swimsuits. Kissing them. Kissing them. At bedtime.

"What in the hell are you nailing up?" he shouts at me.

He is home from work early. I am caught with twenty-two nails, big ones, hammered in, some crooked, some straight, into his ear. He surprises me. I jump. But I have steadier nerves than Mother.

"Hammering nails is a new therapy we've been trying in our group. Releases tension. Helps me to focus. I feel better already." I smile up at him as he studies me, studies my intentions nailed up twenty-two different ways.

"Don't ruin all that good lumber. It's damned expensive." His eyes jerk over me, cold, like he is looking at me through ice. "You're damned expensive."

He always says this when I mention my therapy group.

Mother made cookies. That was her therapy. She found the recipe in a ladies' magazine. Frustration Cookies. A simple recipe of flour and loads of butter, like shortbread. You pound them, the recipe says. Pound, pound, pound them. The more you pound, the better they taste. The more you pound, the better you feel.

Mother let me help. We pounded the dough, together, on a wooden board. The dough gets lighter and whiter. Never black and blue like you would expect. Daddy eats them all. He smiles. We feel better.

He is inside the kitchen. I hear the top pop off a beer can, the sound of the TV comes out the screen door. The rattle of newspapers. The smell of baloney and cheese. I can see everything he does, even when I am not looking.

Mother believed in therapy. She learned assertiveness training, but she never learned how to say, *NO!*

I have learned to watch.

Learning to drive nails is not easy. I have tried all sizes. Thin and long is best, the magazine says. But they bend easily. I try big and little hammers from his tool chest. I balance them in my hand.

Daddy says the art of driving nails is in the flick of the wrist. He tries to teach me, but I do not want to learn.

My wrist hurts. I take a break. I eat a naval orange.

I should not be hammering wood, I tell myself, looking at the navel orange I am eating. Peeling and eating it, a lobe at a time. Peeling it with my finger in its ear. I am all wrong. The ear is soft and spongy, not hard, not like pounding planks.

I go to the grocery to buy navel oranges. The checkout man makes a joke. "Got a craving for navels, huh."

He winks at me like he knows. His eyes follow the ruffles bouncing on my little girls' dresses out the electric doors. *He bears careful watching.*

I take home two ten-pound sacks of Navel oranges. Nothing else.

I kill them all. One after the other, pounding them through their soft, rubbery ears, pounding into their soft brains with a flick of my wrist, with my hammer and a long, thin nail, with their ears turned up to me out of the white pillow.

The magazine did not tell me he would jerk like a live wire fallen into water, that he would jump and jerk and then fall into a naked heap like a rumpled blanket on top of the bed.

Too late. The fifth of Johnny Walker is empty on the bed stand. I make sure. I put on my clothes.

I keep the girls in the kitchen. I give them a bowl of Cheerios and milk. "You can eat supper in peace tonight. You can sleep in peace tonight," I tell them. They stare at me, silently, from behind their bowls. Their eyes float on the milk. Their spoons are pointing. Pointing.

"I tried to get him awake," I tell the ambulance driver. "I shook him. He would not wake up. He drank the bottle dry. All at once. Down, down in big swallows.

Mother? Mother? Mother?

The ambulance driver chews gum with his mouth open. He nods without looking at me. Writes on a clipboard. *Possible alcohol poisoning.*

I watch his writing out of the corner of my eye.

The ambulance driver and another man bring in a plank bed on wheels. He is very still. His head is crooked on his pillow. His eyes are open, floating up white like dead minnows.

The magazine is right. There is nary a drop of blood.

Jamie Baily

Seeds

The orange trees blossom in the winter
in southern Spain.
I went there to escape
the brutality of my life.
There, the Mediterranean is soft and cool and glassy.
And the beaches are filled with fishermen and lovers,
searching for treasure.
I found myself.
But I wanted more.

In Rome, the structures are ancient
and crumbling and precious.
It's unfathomable,
what they have survived
and the secrets they hold.
I stood in front of them,
next to tourists searching for history.
I made peace with my own.
Still, I wanted more.

In Vienna, symphonies spring eternal from the music hall.
In Granada, gypsies busk on the streets,
begging for coins against the background
of a grand castle.
Asking for more.

In Venice, canals run through the city like veins.
Buildings sit shakily on stilts,
as unsure as I am about it all.

In Prague, time marches on in the clock tower.
Smoke over spires.
Bridges upon bridges.
I let them burn.

I returned home to West Virginia,
with its lush, green hills
punctured with white steeples
into the lilac skies.

Where Mamaws and Papaws make breakfast
for the grandkids they are raising.
Prayers flow like water.
The church people,
who watched me root and grow and blossom,
petals scattering away into the open sky,
comment on the strangeness of my presence.
As if I chose the world over this place.

Dana Malone

The only North I ever knew

Remember these words sings the Blue Ridge Mountain pass.
                              The mountain pass says
Write them on yourself.
Your lily legs the only
paper. Stencil of Boaz.

Be not afraid   repeats the mountain pass.
This Kanuga Road
you drive will wind you
into what to say.

Berea, Berea   breathes the Blue Ridge Mountain pass.
Oh your soul
and all within you.   The mountain pass sings

Memory swims
the French Broad currents
where you cast your burdens.

Mt. Mitchell my crown   proclaims the mountain pass
Peak of your Appalachia.
All my water
over each of my rocks
the sweetest song.

I offer you Pisgah Forest   utters the mountain pass.
Camelot with fern carpet.
Crackle of Christ
on the AM dial. Listen   prompts the mountain pass

hear the local quartet intone
Lord plant my feet. Oh how
could heaven be any higher?

Embedded in these slopes
of your salvation   cries the Blue Ridge Mountain pass
are these minerals
of your distant kin.

Serpentine   said the mountain pass
this ink of you.

And how could heaven be any higher?

Dana Malone

Divorce Decree

After stomach churn &
wrangle with sheets all night

there's breath work to be done
friends who do not tell me

I told you so &
breakfast at almost-noon.

Today I peeled a boiled egg.
Shell and skin only.

Every bite waiting, intact.

S. Renay Sanders

Ruby's Baby

May heard a car barreling down the dirt road. She grabbed the dish towel and dried her hands as she made her way to the window to see who was causing that fog of dust. They didn't get a lot of company back in Burrows Cove so all arrivals were noteworthy. The car stopped on the other side of the creek as all cars did since this was the end of the road. There was no bridge across the creek. You had to walk the footpath the rest of the way to the house. Her Daddy liked to say, "There was one road in and one road out."

When the dust settled May recognized the car of her brother Samuel. What was he doing here this time of day? If he was here to help Daddy out in the fields he should have been here hours ago. Daddy would have a fit, him a showing up now. He wouldn't be of much use here in the heat of the day; it was almost time for dinner. In fact, she better get back to cooking because Daddy and them would be in to eat soon and she best have it on the table. Still, she had to find out what Samuel was doing here. Then it struck her, the baby. Surely, he wasn't here because of the baby, it's too soon. Ain't it? Well, she had heard the two grandmas, Mama and Ruby's Mama, Lena, talking after church; they said that baby could come any day now, but today? May hadn't thought it would be today.

Ruby wasn't much older than May and even though at 15 May knew she was pretty well grown she couldn't imagine having a baby. It wasn't that long ago she and Ruby had been playing like they were Mamas with doll babies. She was thrilled when Ruby and Sam got to courting. When they got married it made her and Ruby like sisters. Now on this day, Ruby and Sam was about to have a baby? May could hardly believe it. She had been around when the stock had babies, calves, piglets, and the like but she was usually shooed away at the time of the actual birth. She sure would like to be there when her little niece or nephew came into the world. Reckon Mama would let her come? She could help if Mama told her what to do.

As the car came roaring down the road, Maggie, May's mother, was working in the garden. It was nigh on to twelve o'clock, too hot for working in the sun. She would pick a mess of beans for dinner and then head on up to the house. She'd help May get dinner on the table before Will come in from the field. She had just stopped to get a drink and was returning the dipper to the bucket when she heard the car a coming. She knew, had felt it ever since she got up this morning, that baby was a coming today. She was not surprised when she heard the car. She expected it to be Samuel. May met him on the footlog, determined she was right about the baby; off they went Sam just a flying up that dirt road. She was going to help bring another youngin' into the world. She wasn't attending this birth just as the grandmother, she was going as the midwife too.

Nurse and midwife had been her role in this valley for many a year. Not in a formal sense. She didn't work out of a clinic, didn't hold any degree or license, but she was often called to tend to somebody when they was bad off sick or to help out when somebody was having a baby. She'd learned from her mother and Granny. Though nobody talked about it much, Granny was part Cherokee and knew all the Indian ways. Maggie just took to it had a natural talent for healing. Early on Maggie's Mama left the tending of Maggie's brothers and sisters to her whenever any of them got sick. It wouldn't be long until the neighbors got to calling for her when somebody was sick. If they was really bad off Doc Carter would come too. He'd show Maggie what to do. Wasn't no time until he got to calling for her when babies was being born. What she hadn't learned from her Mama and Granny she learned from the doctor. Doc Carter delivering a baby was a sight. He was a short little man and usually had to get up on a stool to tend to the mother, but he knew his stuff and Maggie was proud to learn from him. Sometimes Doc Carter made it for the births, sometimes he didn't; either way, Maggie did what needed to be done.

Maggie had helped Lena with all of her births. She had been there when Ruby was born. Maggie remembered, Lena let out a couple of deep breaths whew, whew and there was Ruby. After Ruby, Lena barely even grunted when her last few children was born almost slept through the whole thing. Maggie had nine youngins of her own—not quite as many as Lena. She never had quite the easy time Lena had, but she got through it. Now she would help Ruby bring this littlin' into the world.

She knew women in town had got to going to the hospital to have their babies, but as a practical matter, women out in the country had their youngins at home. Hospitals were so far away and not everybody had a car. What if you didn't make it in time? Having a baby at home sure seemed better than having one in the car or on the side of the road. She remembered Granny, talking about babies being born out in the field in her time. Well, this precious child, her grandchild would be born at home. She hadn't been this excited about tending a birth in a long time. She was in the car in no time flat, fogging down the road with Samuel. While it was likely to be a long time before that baby made its way into this world, you couldn't be sure. Babies had their own way of telling time. Best to hurry to get to Ruby. Thank goodness, May was there to fix dinner so she could just take off.

May hung up the cloth she'd been drying her hands-on and headed out, the screen door slamming behind her. She all but ran to the garden; still, she was just in time to see the car pulling away, dust a fogging. It must be the baby; Mama wouldn't have left like that without saying a word. No dinner on the table. May headed back to the house. Nothing to do now but finish up dinner. She was taking the cornbread out of the oven when she noticed her mother's good shoes sitting by the door. Her Mama had run off in her field boots full of garden dirt, manure, and who knows what else. May was sure Mama would want her good shoes. Using this as her excuse to being there when the baby was born, May grabbed up the shoes, found a clean apron, and took off walking down the road to take these things to her Mama. It was a good five-mile walk to her brother and sister-in-law's house, but she was used to long walks. She walked to Cleve Hamby's store just about every week bringing milk for him to sell. Sam and Ruby lived just a stone's throw from the store so she headed out. She'd left dinner on the table for her Daddy. She hadn't waited to tell him about the baby and the shoes for fear he would've stopped her from coming. She figured, with her and Mama gone he would suppose it was the baby's time to come. He would've heard the car coming and going. She hoped and worried that she would get there in time for the birth. She wasn't going to be shooed away this time.

She was just about there when she heard the awfullest sounds. Bellowing and grunting. One of the cows must've got caught up in the fence or something. As she got closer she realized the noise was coming from the house. She'd never heard such sounds from a person before. Surely that noise wasn't coming out of Ruby. The noise settled down as she walked on toward the house. When she got close she heard Ruby say, "Oh shoot, here comes another pain," and then the hollering started again. Oh Lord, when they played house pretending to have husbands and babies, they'd never imagined anything like that. When May got there Lena was a sitting on the porch. When she saw May's frightened face she said: "Oh Ruby's just a scared it's not so bad." May handed Lena the shoes and the apron. She'd lost all thought of helping; she'd just stay there on the porch until the baby was born.

Susan Powers

What Ever You Feel (Song)

What ever you feel I can't ignore
You push, you pull then you let me go
I stared at the earrings left on a shelf
Somehow now I feel like someone else
Who lived a long, long time ago
I'm not the only mother who doesn't know

We've come so far but I let you go
Ask for too much it's not an equal load
I don't know how to mend this broken fence
And the line that it represents
Till you arrive walking through the door
Carrying your childhood like an offering of gold

Susan Powers

Letters from Eden (Song)

Medicine in a bottle don't say goodbye
I don't want to die with a broken heart
Just like Jesse James put down your guns
There's a light in Edenborn tonight

My hands are dirty can't keep them clean
And my mind is dirty and I can't sleep
I was trying to keep my babies fed
No I haven't seen rock bottom yet

You made me believe that you're no good
Try to make me leave you know it's understood
That you love me but it's not enough
The light in Edenborn is dying out

Maybe I'll write a letter home.
No apology address unknown
Took me a lifetime to understand
That love exists in a promise land.

Medicine in a bottle don't cry tonight
Letters from Eden will still arrive
All the love from long ago will make it right
There's a light in Edenborn tonight

Kelly Hanwright

Eye of Fire

Right now,
sitting in your car, take off
those dark glasses, look
yourself in your flaming
eye. Recall,
I am a lioness. Feel
the burning deep beneath
the bruises, sense
the warrior he can't beat
out of you.

Jonie McIntire

How to Protect Yourself When You're Young

Urinate
afterwards, every time.
Wash. Rinse.
Tiptoe back
to bed.

Keep a journal
small enough
to hide.

If you need to get
away during
the day,
nobody checks
the attic,
under the downstairs
bathroom sink,
the top shelf in
grandma's
bedroom
closet.

Keep yourself
small enough
to hide.

Wash
all fingerprints
off. Keep
your bruises
only skin deep.

Shei Sanchez

Into These Woods, I Go

Hey,
I'm boot-deep in snow. My toes blue
& aching for this piece of land
outside the city of six-sided clay bricks, laid

long before I decided to plant
these wandering feet on them, before
this hardened heart was stamped

with country ink, tree-purled
& stitched with breathless
undulations my urban blood

hungers for, even
on this cold-drenched day
– a surprise

for a kid born on concrete:
alleys and water towers, now
hollows and creeks, zooming

train currents, now gusts
from ridge tops. I traded my Doc Martens
for these plain mud boots,

the shiny windows and malls high
on a/c for white oaks that whisper,
whisper, when I stand still for the scent

of burning wood on my hair. Do you miss
your past life? Would you want it back
when you're grayer than these sullen winter

skies? Tomorrow, I'll bury my city
grime again, with one old shirt over another,
a pair of pants pocked with thorn pricks, dive

into these woods, & go.

Shei Sanchez

First Born

Like a moth and her lamplight, this little one
   looks for a bosom. Before he could
   barely stand on his own, legs trembling

like saplings in a storm, his mouth motions
   toward his momma. A mandible on a muzzle
   smelling for the scent of home. Just minutes ago,

his snout, with nostrils pulsing awake,
   emerged with small front hoofs, followed by
   the rest of him, pushed out of her—

slick, lithesome, whole. I held him, my arms
   instantly stiffening into a poor man's palanquin.
   My heart softened like sunrise, tears brimming

in the corners where blood and light meet.
   Was I just witness to a meaning of life?
   This is the closest I will come to being

a mother. Holding a breathing body dependent
   on another breathing body. His warmth, the closest
   thing to touching a star. My own body dependent

on modern medicine to survive. She called out to him,
   her first born, this wonder of a creature, so alive,
   so daring. His first cry, an assertion to matter

in this world. When do we lose our way
   from the wild? His cloven feet find ground
   for his first forage, mother's manna,

colostrum to flourish. She bathes him
   with her tongue, unearthing fur
   fine as the powder of moth wings.

He struggles to latch.
   I struggle to help him.
   Two animals trying to thrive.

Patricia Thrushart

What Passes For Dew

Come back when the eggplant is
cerise and white,
hiding its carnival stripes beneath
rippled umbrella leaves;
the last of the peas have burst, their
deep-throated flowers a memory;
the bee has had its fill of
pollen, and drowses on the fragrant fringe
of a nodding herb.

The insects call to you, high in the oaks,
their thrum a drumming of the sacred
circle—sun and moon, wet and sparse,
cold and now, this time,
drenched in heat and heavy air,
dripping with what passes for dew.

You know you belong here, don't you? As surely as the vireo
who sings about home incessantly,
knowing how heavenly it is,
knowing how easily
it is lost.

Patricia Thrushart

Knee Highs

We wore them with our
plaid-pleated skirts hemmed
to cover the knees,
stiff gabardine jackets
to cover our breasts,
a pinned-on kleenex
to cover our hair
if we forgot the veil for Mass.

Our Mary Janes were never
patent leather—
the nuns warned us
how well they reflect
upward.

After school on the bus
those of us
who were precocious
rolled up our skirts,
pushed down our socks,
exposing thighs and calves
firm from running
through back-yard fields of corn,
knee-high by the Fourth of July,
when we'd be free of uniforms,
and notebooks,
and nuns
who could explain the reflective quality
of patent leather
but never
mentioned the back seat of a boy's car,
or rolled-up mary jane between the lips,
or how some men liked pictures
of playful school girls
in hiked-up, pleated skirts
with thin, ribbed
knee highs,

and nothing else.

Kathy Guest
Face of Time

Danielle Kelly

Out of Jordan

Route thirty-three drug on for miles. Maria had the curves of the land memorized, or at least between Jordan Valley and Dixon. Fairly new, the route's original design was to link Washington, D.C. directly to West Virginia, but still sections of the road North of Jordan Valley barred cars from entering. William accelerated around the first mountain and Maria leaned against the turn, her hand holding the postcard firm against the seat. She had believed Jake would contact her, but until she saw the postcard in the mailbox last night, she hadn't realized she had given up on him.

Clouds moved in and a leaf tornado spun on the berm created by the coal truck ahead of them. William sped up as if he could help push the truck up the steep mountain, but Maria had learned some things were impossible. She picked up the postcard, held it firmly in her hands so the wind didn't carry it away through the cracked window behind them. She didn't even think postcards were a thing anymore. Most people emailed or called. But Jake wasn't typical or easy. When they were little, she and Jake would sit outside in the yard and make up constellations, connecting the stars with their fingertips until a shape was formed or until their mom called them inside to go to bed. Now, Maria wondered if Jake would have approved of the new shape her life had become.

"You're going to have to read that eventually," William said.

"I know. I've waited for six months to get answers about—" she trailed off. Jake had left in the middle of the night. At seventeen, he'd packed his bags and disappeared without telling a single one of them— Maria, her parents, even their closest cousin Colleen—where he was going.

"Sometimes you got to let people live their own lives." He reached over to grab her hand. His fingernails were coated in oil from the garage where he worked. The grease coated her skin kind of like armor, but it felt more like a slimy film she could never wash away.

Static filled Maria's silence. When they reached Boy Scout Camp road the local Presbyterian service filtered through the speakers with "amens" and "do you believes". Maria believed she'd never find a boy willing to look at her twice, which is why she had agreed to move-in with William only months after they started dating. She'd only said yes because it was the first time any boy besides her brother, Jake, had noticed her as more than who she was: a Jordan Valley girl desperate to get out of the valley and of herself.

When they finally reached William's house, the road narrowed. Tree limbs from the morning storm rattled underneath them. Although she had seen the trailer a few times, she hadn't seen it in the daylight. It wasn't much. An odd shade of green that stuck out from the grass and trees that surrounded them. Five cinderblocks stacked crooked led to the front door. The least he could have done was invest in some two by fours and cement to make the steps more welcoming, but she didn't have the energy to pick a fight tonight. When she got out of the car, she stepped straight into a giant mud puddle. Perfect.

Inside, she kicked off her shoes while the screen door slammed behind her. The windows were bare, no blinds or bed sheets to block out the sun. To the left, an old TV sat on the countertop that split the kitchen from the living space. She placed the postcard on the counter, wedging the corner under the TV for safekeeping.

"It's not much. But it will do for a little while, until I open up my own shop," William said. He sat down on what looked like a futon and patted the space beside him.

"Thanks," she said, sitting beside him. "For everything."

Before she had time to think, William had slipped his hands under her shirt and pressed his body against hers until she thought the back of the futon would fall from the force of their bodies now against it. Her hands followed his lead getting adjusted to his rhythm: under the shirt, around the chest, down, stop at the waistband of his pants. She didn't have time to think or stop or speak up, so instead she pretended that she was somewhere else. Someone else. Someone who knew how this all worked.

When they were done, she excused herself to the bathroom to wash off. From the bathtub, she could see her entire naked body in the mirror. Her brown hair had dulled and stopped abruptly at her chin. Her stomach created folds where they shouldn't be. She could still feel his hands knead the folds and find his way to her, yet she didn't know how William had made love to her with all this excess being around her.

She wasn't supposed to be loved. That's what she had decided after Jake left her to pick up the pieces. He'd never let her run off with a guy like William. When Maria was finally old enough to date, Jake told her that no boy was ever good enough for her. At the time she thought he was just being the protective slightly, older brother, but, now she knew that he had only acted that way because no boy would even want to slip their hands beneath her blouse. Fat. Plump. Plus size. The labels were many. Whatever label people gave her, it didn't matter because they all meant the same thing: unlovable. Then William came along one evening into the Rite Aid where she worked, his coal black hair slicked back to his shoulders and his shirt puckered in the middle. At the time, her cousin Colleen, who worked alongside Maria, had nudged her to go along with him. "What can it hurt?" Colleen had said. It couldn't, Maria had thought, but now, as she got out of the shower, all she worried about was how this postcard from Jake would affect her.

"What are you doing?" William leaned against the bathroom doorway.

"Washing up. It's been a long day."

"Sure has. Your clothes are in the bedroom, if you need them." He handed her a towel.

"Thanks." She wrapped the towel around her body.

"So?" he asked.

"So what?"

"That was—"

"Listen, you don't have to—"

"Great."

"Yeah right."

"Babe," he said. His hand moved toward her and the towel. "Let me love you. That's all I'm asking."

Love. The word hung between them for the first time. She wasn't even sure what love meant or should feel like with William. Things were fun most of the time, but she wasn't ready to let anyone else in her life that could hurt her. Maria stepped out of the tub and walked away.

Later, after William had gone to bed, Maria stumbled to the kitchen for the postcard, then walked outside, sitting on the cool cinderblocks, the porch light dull above her. She timed her breath to the breeze carrying the leaves into the night sky. It was darker here. If that was even possible. She spent most of her childhood afraid of the dark, but out here she felt safer than being inside. Then she took out the postcard, the edges already curled.

She turned the card over in her hands and for the first time she really looked at it. A field of dandelions filled the front, all of them bent back in a field as if their seeds were waiting to scatter with the next wind. *Wishing Flower,* Jake had scrawled at the top. Their mom said dandelions carried wishes out into the world at just the right moment whenever the wishes needed to be heard. Not until the flowers turned white, were the wishes sent out by a strong wind or a warm breath.

On the backside, she searched the postmark but it was illegible. It could be Illinois. Maybe Indiana. Or a field in Idaho. All places she had never been and would probably never see. His message was simple: "This reminded me of you, sis."

And like that, the postcard ended. No "see you soon" or "miss you." She hugged her knees as the wind picked up. Dammit. She wished she were sitting in the field of dandelions with Jake beside her. She wished she had stopped him before he left town. Spoke up. Told him she loved him when she watched him kiss another guy. He had given her that much all her life, a voice, a place to belong and feel comfortable. Why couldn't she have done the same thing?

In front of her, a firefly dipped towards her and she reached out and trapped it in her hand. The light broke through the cracks of her fingers. "It's okay. I won't hurt you," she whispered to the bug trapped inside her hand. She swished the words on her tongue. They tasted like Jordan Valley. Stale. Rotten. Bittersweet. The light in her hand dulled until everything went dark again leaving her to wonder if the light truly existed.

Leslie Clark

Testament

When I was born, my mother loved me at first sight.
"Isn't she beautiful? What's her name?" she asked.
The doctor and the nurse smiled kindly she recalled.
My father was in Korea at the time.

"Isn't she beautiful? What's her name?" she asked.
No one knew when my father would return.
My father was in Korea at the time.
My mother held me close and kissed my head.

No one knew when my father would return.
Life is seldom what you expected it to be.
My mother held me close and kissed my head.
I nestled into her comforting embrace.

Life is seldom what you expected it to be.
I grew up with a sense of absolute love.
I nestled into her comforting embrace.
I've never wished for anything as much.

I grew up with a sense of absolute love.
The doctor and the nurse smiled kindly she recalled.
I've never wished for anything as much.
When I was born, my mother loved me at first sight.

Jayne Moore Waldrop

Ballast

You were warned
the journey wouldn't be easy.
Orange diamonds bobbed
along your chosen route.
Like a captain sailing
with too much ballast
you learned to cast aside
dead weight
lest they drag you down.
At times you panicked,
jettisoned too much,
then listed and leaned,
nearly heeled over,
before righting yourself
and moving on.
The debris field grew wide,
littered with your jetsam,
valuables once loved
yet intentionally discarded
as you saved yourself.
From a distance
abandoned property
churning in your wake
looked like mere specks
before they sank to the bottom,
got stranded in the muck.
But sometimes those
insignificant fragments
fight the tide and resurface,
gasp for air,
float to a safe sandy shore
to find themselves
polished like sea glass,
transformed into treasure.

Barbara Lyghtel Rohrer

The Road From Longing

"The road was new to me, as roads always are, going back."
—Sarah Orne Jewett

The news that Paul was getting married brought Longing to my door. I recognized it immediately, unlike in the past when I confused it with regret or loss. Longing. What could this yearning tell me?

I first met Longing as a 12-year-old while standing in my backyard one afternoon as a storm moved in. Our house was built at the top of the hill in Dayton, Kentucky, giving a view of the town of Bellevue and, beyond, the Ohio hillside across the river. I felt the wind toss my hair and brush my face. I loved the gray of the sky and sensed its power. I saw how vines curled around the old iron fence, an ornamental section stuck along the edge of the yard between a hedgerow and a section of wire fence. A decorative piece so out of place in my working class neighborhood. Where it came from or how it got there, I did not know. The fence called to me, as if it were an entity, like Longing would someday become for me.

For years, I would turn back to that moment. What was that feeling? So full, as if I touched something I could not know. And I was in awe of its beauty. That may have been the first time I merged in my psyche an emotion or an unconscious sense with a physical object. That iron fence represented that experience for me, came to represent Longing itself, though it would be years before I would tease that into a frame of understanding.

In my twenties, I was in a relationship with a man 20 years my senior. Don owned a farmhouse about 75 miles east of Cincinnati, Ohio, nestled near Serpent Mound. Our mailing address was Peebles, Ohio, the closest town, but Hillsboro, west of us, was larger, was where we shopped and so I identified more with that community. While I was with Don, I always kept an apartment in the Cincinnati area, but for the most part I lived with him on his 30 acres of land. We had a garden, and I learned to can. We raised chickens. We kept honeybees—and sold the honey commercially.

I spent time walking the woods that flanked the house. There was much there that was good, but there was also pain and loneliness. Don and I were not building anything together. I was simply living with him on his property. I longed for intimacy, but that was not possible in that relationship. Don had his limitations, but so did I. I could not create with him what I yearned for.

During those years, I fell under the allure of Hillsboro. It stood for me as all that was good about small towns. I saw community and the

194

opportunity for a simpler life: backyard gardens, a library and post office within walking distance; a smart dress shop with an adorable sundress that I could not afford; a fabric store with remnants that I could afford. There was a cafe with the best biscuits and gravy and a little sidewalk creamery with my favorite mint chocolate chip ice cream. I saw myself living there, inviting friends over for dinner. And, yes, I saw possibilities for intimacy.

Some twenty years later, two visionaries began building a community of trees, about 20 minutes east of Hillsboro, on the Rocky Fork Gorge. Their purpose was to rebuild a swath of wilderness, a sanctuary. I was one of many who stepped forward in support of this endeavor, which eventually came to be the Arc of Appalachia Preserve System. This is where I met Paul—a doll of a young man with long dark hair. He came to the sanctuary as a college intern and stayed. *If only I were 25 years younger,* I thought.

I heard of Paul's upcoming marriage as I was volunteering at the Arc for its annual wildflower pilgrimage. I gave him my blessings and wished him well. He had been an integral part of a place I love, and now he would be moving north with his bride. His departure awakened Longing in me for what I was never able to build with a man.

In the past at such moments, I would have stepped into the regret of the choices I have made and the life I have not lived. But that day, I was following Longing to see where it would take me. I knew something deeper was stirring and the waters had yet to clear.

After completing my morning stint as part of the pilgrimage's breakfast crew, I headed to the creek that cuts through the Rocky Fork Gorge and slipped my kayak into the waters. I love hiking the trails of the Arc, but I consider these waters to be the heart of the sanctuary. That day, I passed two mother geese sitting on their eggs atop grassy boulders near the water's edge. White trilliums and Virginia bluebells grew along the banks I floated by. The craggy faces of rock cliffs gazed down on me in my little blue boat. I was paddling in paradise.

At one point, my eyes were drawn to sunlit white waters spilling down a cut in the rock, like a waterfall from heaven. I tried to slow my boat to absorb the image, wanting to hold it and not let it go. But the creek pulled me on. Like a teen texting while driving, I wasn't watching where I was going. When I looked up, I saw I was headed into a low hanging branch. I tried to lift it overhead, but the branch would not budge. It took me out. Over I rolled into the waters. I was baptized anew.

Later, in dry clothes, I wandered over to the house on Briar Hill. Some of the properties that the Arc has been able to purchase have houses that are offered to land stewards. Briar Hill was one of those properties. It had an old schoolhouse that a couple had converted into a home to live in until the end of their days. Land stewards buy houses such as Briar Hill for the

Arc with a life-long right of residency. The land stewards get a tax deduction, while the sanctuary expands its holdings. Briar Hill was available for land steward purchase.

When I walked into the Briar Hill house, I could see the shabbiness of its rough floors and bare walls, its warped cabinets and rusty porcelain. But I also saw the alcove with a little bench by the front door. I saw the built-in corner cabinets with glass doors in the dining room. I saw wall panels with scored rectangles in the bedroom. At one time it had been a sweet home. A stairwell rose up from the four rooms on the first floor to a large open space on the second floor, sloped walls and all. The space would make a nice writing studio, I thought. I knew the whole house could be lovely once again—with much work and far more dollars than I had. *I will never own this place,* I thought. Surprisingly, I accepted that thought with ease.

Still I ached with Longing.

And Longing is what I rode home with later that day. My route back took me, as it always does, straight through Hillsboro. I picked up Route 138 west out of town. The miles gave plenty of space for thought.

What did Hillsboro represent for me—and the Arc by extension? My mind returned to Don, the man who brought me to this area, and what hadn't been possible between us. Did Hillsboro represent what was not possible?

When I left Don, I left the town of Hillsboro. Now my work with the Arc has me returning again and again. It has me returning to my Longing.

"The thing that I call living is just being satisfied." I have always liked that line from Gordon Lightfoot's "Carefree Highway." To be satisfied sounded like a way to live a life that had depth and meaning. But as the miles rolled by that day I drove home from the Arc, I saw that there was a place for Longing too. It was a place that I needed to touch again and again.

I pulled into my driveway where my house, a Cape Cod, sits on the end of a cul-de-sac in a suburban community just east of Cincinnati. It was late in the afternoon. Birds were calling and flitting about. Trees in the woods that line my property stirred against the blue sky. Their leaves were so young and fresh that their green color had a yellow cast in the sunlight. The grass was shaggy and thick, and heavily sprinkled with dandelions. In the side yard, two dirty white Adirondack chairs waited for me to sit a spell. The colors were as vivid as a postcard. I liked what I saw. I got out of the car and walked inside.

I looked at my comfortable living room with walls my nephew painted a forest green. I walked into the kitchen I had just helped my brothers remodel with new maple cabinets and a bamboo floor framed with dark red walls. Upstairs in a butter yellow studio with sloped walls, I had essays waiting to be completed. And with that, Longing left.

I realized that Hillsboro represented my longing, as well as what was not possible in my life. *Once.* I thought how just because something was not possible now, does not mean it is impossible forever. And the deeper I had gone into that feeling of longing, the wider that reality became. I saw how my longings could be met in more than one way. And while I could not have voiced it this way at the time, it was as if I knew, as a dear friend would later say, that accepting what I had was not giving up, but opening up.

And for those longings that will never be satisfied, I have the purity of desire—and that too has a purpose. I will always have longings that are greater than what I have or am. I need these longings to push me on, like the current of the river. Who knows what I'll find just around the bend.

Now when I drive through Hillsboro, I touch that longing. It feeds me, like good food, a pleasant evening with friends, the rain on my skylight, all things I enjoy but none of which I would want to go on endlessly. Likely I will never go through Hillsboro without feeling longing. But I know now that this is not to live unsatisfied. *Longing is part of what makes my life whole.*

I walked through my Cape Cod again, more slowly this time. It is a house that in many ways resembles the old schoolhouse on Briar Hill. If Hillsboro represented my longing, it also was my blindness. Despite a clear plan, I wasn't realizing the desires of my heart. I hadn't been able to see what I had created.

I knew then why I was comfortable with the thought that I will never own the house on Briar Hill, why I could let go of that dream so easily. I did not need to buy and re-model the Briar Hill house. I already had. I was standing in it.

Marlene L'Abbé
Down Under

Pauletta Hansel

Postcard from Age 60

Most mornings I unspool the knotted rope of me
into cool water, trying to dip down
into gratitude. My sinking body
in its nylon suit still moves as I tell it to,
the lift and push of limbs across the length of pool.
Mother, some days I even remember to thank
the ache that lives at the base of my spine, too,
for how it lifts me buoyant to this place of ease.
I am trying to believe it is not the weight,
but how we carry what we're given that bends
us down, or lets us float awhile, suspended
in these years between the gathering up
and letting go. Mother, I am trying
to let go, but not of everything, a soft
loosening of my clench upon this world
I entered through your body.

Pauletta Hansel

This Is the Poem That Has Been Staring
at You for Some Time Now

Remember the night you saw yourself
in the mirror the other side of the bar,
Arnold's 1985, framed between the bottles,
and you were slapped by
your own loveliness, unloved?
That was the poem.
It wanted to ask you
what it was you were
so afraid of.
Now it thinks it knows
the only perfect poem
is the one you would have written
then, and then is never now,
and now is always too soon.
Tonight in the mirror you want
to slap that girl's other cheek,
if you only knew where she was,
wake her up to her life.
But the only perfect happiness
is the one you don't know
is yours.

Pauletta Hansel

Letter to Myself, 15

I am writing to you from the end of the world.
—Henri Michaux, "I Am Writing to You from a Far-Off Country"

I want to tell you how, in time, everything shows on the skin. Today, turning my wrist to bite an apple, I saw a new ridge at the base of my palm. A gentle rise of loosened flesh, not like the sharp slashed mountains where you, in my mind, your only home, remain. Think instead of farmland, river basin, sloped pastures, plowed fields. O, you smooth girl. Broken only by the sharp protrusion of bone you were so proud of—ankle, knee, hip, steep pitch of pelvic cage above the valley. The ridge of ribs. You hungered away the softness. Your power lay not in the just-ripe plums of breast but in the knob between them. What have I done with you? What did you do to me? There is a small scar, a distant lightning bolt, on my right wrist slashed all those years ago by the impatience of the left thumb's jagged nail. Every time I see its raised white welt, I think of the one who hurt me open then, his love—we'll call it that—a scalpel to the other scars you once lifted your body to receive, now invisible beneath the bone. Did you believe if you could hide what did not heal, the hurt would cease to matter? But we are made of matter, girl. And now this body you have left me to begins to show your leaving. Think deer track through the fallow winter field where every step in thawing ground is visible. And I am trying to love this land, mine now to tend.

L. Renée

the bone carrier

my granddaddy used
to tell his children
if somebody'll bring
a bone, they'll take
a bone,
which is to say
gossips always have
need for fresh meat
don't matter which part,
or put another way,
talk with bad intentions
calcifies like any good
femur, the longest
and strongest bone
in the human
body that fastens hip
joint to knee joint,
source of any good
juke joint gyrate
where a good girl
might've heard some bad
rhymes spinning off
the vinyl record
of some jive turkey's
lips and let her hips
fall into the cradle
of that music
and let her knees
drop down beneath
that alter to praise
its fine symmetry,
how everything squares
perfectly when you add
moonshine and moonlight
and guitar strings
striking chords
so deeply in a body
so filled with aching
they feel like nerve-

endings firing
the kind of heat
you don't know
if you can stand,
which makes you want
to stand with it
that much more,
hold the electric fantastic
in the fine circuits
of your diaphysis,
and maybe reach
for the bright plumage
of that jive cock's neck
to stabilize the shaking
pulsing now through
your marrow,
which some unkind observer
might call stock tomorrow,
carrying your midnight
bone to a neighbor's front
porch talkin bout how
your family's good broth
done turned sour.

L. Renée

The Unmapped Place

Here where the ruby-throated cardinal
dips her beak in a cool blue pool,
then flies high to perch her soprano
on a leafy limb that boosts her trilling,

here where song can tell you what
to mourn and what to praise, where many
a day they be the same, grief and gratitude
long-distant cousins, where miracles aren't

welded to stained glass but dive off
lapels framing the one white polyester
suit Mother Franklin sweats through every
first Sunday, singing beneath the sagging

church roof, the cave of her throat reaching
deeply into a pit of sorrows none of us can
see but know are there, pulling up notes
like buckets sloshing with well water,

well-watered tears that drench the ears
with sudden chills, the witnessing of not
knowing how she got over, how she made it
from one Sunday to another Sunday

in her right mind, when the worrying
over what she could afford to lose,
who she could not afford to lose,
consumed every waking thought,

until the words gurgled in that gulf
unintelligible shouts that grown folks
called catching the Holy Ghost,
hand made holy in the reaching,

the lowering down to the sunken place
that has no bottom, no boundary, no way
of knowing how close to the getting
over you are, your proximity to that

opening that lifts you high, the invisible
phantom limb suddenly a Go-Go Gadget
Hand boosting the body out and up,
slackened from the muck, the spiritual

body far-flung, sprung loose enough
to survey the impossibility of earth,
the red soles of brown feet that molded
red clay, how those souls birthed paths

with nothing more than blood and foot
calluses, blessed assurances, how the leaves
exhaled clearings from their native trees
rooted deep in dirt before well-built wells,

waiting for us to remember our way
back to those kin, like Mother Franklin,
back to the unmapped place where they wait
dwelling on perches we still can sing from —

L. Renée

Tradition

By Saturday afternoon the stovetop needed rest,
but Mama said there's no rest for the weary.

By then her hands had already pressed
spatulas into skillets of sizzling bacon,

cheesy scrambled eggs, and Granny Smiths
softening their sour peels in a pool

of butter, brown sugar, a cloud
of cinnamon and nutmeg crackling.

This was our tradition. Full bellies
after cleaning the apartment until it reeked

of Clorox bleach, until windows were Windexed
almost as transparent as air, but ours

tinged fake pine tart as if cardboard
trees hung bright green from the newly

glossed wood furniture. And still, her hands
pressed on, untangling my two-week-old braids

soiled with playground sweat, dandelion dust,
fuzzy wayward wisps left by an Ohio wind's

kiss as I flung my blue-barretted head back
to predict the precise velocity

my hand needed to pummel a tetherball
so fast a sucka kid wouldn't have time enough

to interfere with its perfect spiral,
like the curled hair I longed for. Mama scratched

my scalp clean with French-tipped nails
in the kitchen sink bubbles,

foaming away stories of my days
she always asked about. I sat in the back

of our 1987 Ford Mercury after Latchkey
and her long paralegal shifts, the navy box

on wheels barely putt-putted us home, exhaust
letting out black plumes of smoke and gasps

like gun shots. Mama pressed her foot
down on the pedal to carry us to the weekend

when she cranked up the boombox loud
enough to hear Mary J. Blige crooning

about "Real Love" over the hair dryer
and shellacked my fro with scoops of Royal

Crown petroleum: dressing down the full shaft
of my fluff, wielding the same oak-barreled

pressing comb my Grandmama heated on top
an old coal stove in the kitchen of her mining

camp shack telling my Mama, as my Mama tells me
now, to hold down my ear when she hovers near

my temples, so scorching brass teeth
don't take a bite of my barely-worn skin.

Contributors

Author of the novel *Like Light, Like Music* & the poetry collection *Blood Harmony*, **Lana Austin** is the winner of the Alabama State Poetry Society Book of the Year Award, a Hackney Poetry Award & the Words & Music Poetry Award. Austin has an MFA from GMU & teaches at UAH.

Jamie Bailey is lawyer, writer, and a restless traveler from Southern Ohio. No matter where she roams, her heart lies in the foothills. She is passionate about justice and storytelling, and she is ecstatic when those two passions intersect.

KB Ballentine's seventh collection, *Edge of the Echo*, launched May of 2021 with Iris Press. Her earlier books can be found with Blue Light Press, Middle Creek Publishing, and Celtic Cat Publishing. Her work also appears in anthologies including *Pandemic Evolution* (2021), *In Plein Air* (2017) *and Carrying the Branch: Poets in Search of Peace* (2017). Learn more at www.kbballentine.com.

Tamara M. Baxter's collection of fiction, *Rock Big and Sing Loud*, won the Morehead State's First Author's Award for Fiction, and was published by the Jesse Stuart Foundation with introduction by Robert Morgan. Her work has been published in journals such as *Artemis, Appalachian Review, Now and Then, The Sow's Ear*, and *Women Speak Anthology*, V. 6.

Catherine Carter's most recent poetry collection is *Larvae of the Nearest Stars* (LSU Press, 2019). Her poetry has appeared in *Best American Poetry, Orion, Poetry, Ecotone, RHINO*, and *Ploughshares*, among others. She lives with her spouse in Cullowhee, North Carolina, and is a professor of English at Western Carolina University.

Catherine Pritchard Childress teaches writing and literature and serves as co-director of the Bert C. Bach Written Word Initiative at East Tennessee State University. Her poems have appeared in *North American Review, The Cape Rock, Appalachian Review, and Still: The Journal*. She is the author of the poetry collection *Other* (Finishing Line Press, 2015).

Leslie Clark was born in West Virginia and now lives in Cincinnati, Ohio. She draws creative inspiration from people, nature and the quirks of life. Her chapbook, *Driving in the Dark*, was published in 2017. Her poems have appeared in *Pine Mountain Sand & Gravel* and WOAP *Women Speak*, 2020.

Mary Lucille DeBerry grew up in Harrisville, West Virginia, and spent most of her working years as a public television producer/director at WWVU-TV—later WNPB-TV. Since retirement, she has published a trilogy of poetry collections: *Bertha Butcher's Coat* (2009); *Alice Saw the Beauty* (2014); and *She Was the Girl* (2020).

Born and raised in western North Carolina, **Angelyn DeBord** grew up in the midst of her extended family. Her publications include *Women in American*

Theater; A Gathering at the Forks, An Anthology; Listen Here, Women Writing in Appalachia; Journal of Appalachian Studies; Winds #94, The Hindman Edition; Southern Appalachian Storytellers. Her paintings are inspired by her family and by the colorful images surrounding her: the magical mountains where she has always lived, mason jars full of beets, grapes and peaches, clothes hanging on a line, and soft old fabric patched into abstract designs.

Kate Madia Dieringer was born and raised in West Virginia, has worked as a trauma and sexual violence response nurse, is a graduate of the Writer's Studio Program at Simon Fraser University and lives in Malawi.

Cecile Dixon is a retired ED nurse who, after a thirty-year sojourn to Ohio, has returned to her beloved Kentucky hills to write and raise goats. Cecile holds an MFA from Bluegrass Writers Studio. Her work has been published in *Dead Mule School of Southern Literature, Fried Chicken and Coffee, Pine Mountain Sand and Gravel, Still: the Journal, KY Herstory.*

The granddaughter of coal miners, **Mitzi Dorton** takes inspiration from the strong oral tradition of storytelling in her family. She wrote her first poem at seven. Dorton has been published in literary journals and anthologies, to include *Rattle*, (Appalachian Poets) and *Proud to Be*, Southeast Missouri State University Press.

Ellis Elliott is a writer, ballet teacher, and writing group leader. She lives in Juno Beach, FL with her husband and has a blended family of 6 young men. She has been published in *Signal Mountain Review, Literary Mama, Evening Street Press*, and others.

Julie M. Elman is a professor in the School of Visual Communication at Ohio University, where she teaches courses in publication design, and editorial illustration. Before landing at OU, Elman worked in the newspaper industry as a visual journalist. Elman's book *Fear, Illustrated: Transforming What Scares Us*, was published in 2017.

Alyson Annette Eshelman's Appalachian heritage and faith has guided her creative outlet. Maintaining a home studio, she continues to create new works for exhibitions and accepts commissions for private and religious collections. Eshelman has participated extensively in solo, group, and juried exhibitions, receiving numerous awards for her work.

CJ Farnsworth is a poet residing in WV and a graduate of the Vermont College of Fine Arts MFA Program. Her poems have been published in several print and online publications, including *Community College Humanities Review Journal, Women Speak, Kenning, Kestrel, Poetry Quarterly, Mountain Scribes, and Poetry on the Move*. She is a 2020 Pushcart Prize nominee.

Diana Ferguson, also known as "DiFergi," has been painting and showing art for over thirty years. Currently residing in East Tennessee, she shows regionally and nationally. Her work can be described as lively, whimsical, and layered. Her images lead the viewer on a questioning and emotive visual journey.

Marguerite Floyd is the author of *Everyone's Daughter* (poetry) and three books about parrots. Her poetry has been published in the *Cincinnati Poetry Review, Kentucky Poetry Review, Wind, Cold Mountain Review, Devilfish, American Journal of Nursing, New Flash Fiction, The Poet,* and *Rattle,* as well other magazines and anthologies.

Whitney Folsom grew up in and currently lives in southern Ohio, where she works as a licensed mental health therapist. She utilizes various mediums to portray the amalgamation of beauty and decay, focusing on Appalachian origin, symbolism, and folkloric ritual, primarily through photography and taxidermy.

Kathy Guest is an artist who works with paper as her medium. With a BFA in printmaking from Tyler School of Art, she works to make paper pieces as emotive as paintings. She belongs to an international organization of paper artists and has work in collections in Poland, Bulgaria, and Turkey.

Kari Gunter-Seymour's poetry collections include *A Place So Deep Inside America It Can't Be Seen,* winner of the 2020 Ohio Poet of the Year Award, and *Serving.* Her poems appear in numerous journals including *Verse Daily, Rattle, The NYimes,*and *ONE.* Her photographs have been published in *The Sun, Looking at Appalachia, Appalachian Heritage,* and many others. She a writer-in-residence at the Wexner Center for the Arts and the Poet Laureate of Ohio. Learn more at: www.kariguntersseymourpoet.com

Pauletta Hansel's books include *Friend, Coal Town Photograph* and *Palindrome* (2017 Weatherford Award). *Heartbreak Tree* is forthcoming from Madville Publishing. Her writing was featured in *Oxford American, Verse Daily* and *Poetry Daily.* Pauletta was Cincinnati's first Poet Laureate and is the past managing editor of *Pine Mountain Sand & Gravel.* https://paulettahansel.wordpress.com/.

Kelly Hanwright is the author of *The Locust Years,* a new poetic memoir on growing up with a parent who had undiagnosed schizophrenia. Kelly is a Best-of-the-Net and two-time Pushcart Prize nominee. Her work has appeared in *Birmingham Arts Journal, SoulLit, Heart of Flesh Literary Journal, American Diversity Report,* and more.

Diana Hays grew up in Jackson County, KY. She wrote a history of the roles of Appalachian women as part of her studies at the Goddard-Cambridge Graduate School for Social Change. She is a retired administrator and fundraiser who is learning to write poetry.

Kelli Hansel Haywood is an author, public speaker/workshop guide, mother, and yogi in the mountains of southeastern Kentucky. She is a writer of lived experiences. Her recent publications can be found in the anthology *Appalachian Reckoning: A Region Responds to Hillbilly Elegy,* and *Pine Mountain Sand & Gravel.*

Melissa Helton lives, writes, teaches, and raises her family deep in the

Appalachian Mountains of Kentucky. Her work has appeared or is forthcoming in *Anthology of Appalachian Writers, Shenandoah, Appalachian Review, Still: The Journal*, and more. Her chapbooks include *Inertia: A Study* (2016) and *Hewn* (2021).

Pamela Hirschler grew up in eastern Kentucky, studied creative writing at Morehead State University, and received an MFA in Poetry from Drew University. Her poetry and reviews have previously appeared in *Pine Mountain Sand & Gravel, Still: The Journal, Tupelo Quarterly*, and other journals. Her first poetry chapbook collection, *What Lies Beneath*, was published in 2019 by Finishing Line Press.

Mary Ann Honaker is the author of *Becoming Persephone* (Third Lung Press, 2019) and the chapbooks *It Will Happen Like This* (YesNo Press, 2015) and *Gwen and the Big Nothing* (The Orchard Street Press, 2020.) Mary holds an MFA from Lesley University. She lives in Beaver, West Virginia.

Libby Falk Jones is winner of the 2021 Joy Bale Boone Poetry Prize from *The Heartland Review* and author of a new chapbook, *Yakety Yak (Don't Talk Back)* (Workhorse, 2021). An emerita professor of English at Berea College, Jones co-leads Coming of Age, a writing program for Kentucky women over 60.

Annette Kalandros is a retired teacher, residing in Texas. She was born and raised in Baltimore, MD by a single mother who cherished her West Virginia roots and told stories of her family's struggle there during the Great Depression. Her mother's stories and those of her mother's sister, Christine, influenced who she is and who her daughter will one day become.

Following a nomadic military childhood and decades in northwest Florida's sugar-white sands, **Lisa Kamolnick** traced an ancestral trail and settled in northeast Tennessee's highlands. She holds a B.A. in English from University of Florida. Her work is published or forthcoming in *Tennessee Voices, Black Moon Magazine* and *Mildred Haun Review*.

Danielle Kelly was born and raised in West Virginia, but now resides in Zanesville, OH. She serves as Assistant Professor of English at West Virginia University at Parkersburg. A two-time Pushcart Prize nominee, her work has appeared in *Hedge Apple Magazine, rkvry*, and in *Women Speak* vol. 5.

Stephanie Kendrick is the author of *Places We Feel Warm* (Main Street Rag, 2021) and co-host of Athens County's Thursday Night Open Mic. Her poems have appeared in *Sheila-Na-Gig Online, Women Speak* Volumes 4, 5, & 6, *Still: The Journal, Northern Appalachia Review, Poets Reading the News* and elsewhere. See more at stephthepoet.org.

Natalie Kimbell is a mother of two, and a grandmother of four. She works as a teacher of English, creative theater, and creative writing at her high school alma mater in Dunlap, Tennessee.

Connie Kinsey is a former military brat who has put down deep roots in a converted barn on a dirt road at the top of a hill in West Virginia. She lives with two dogs and a cat, and is pursuing happiness, one cup of coffee at a time.

Patsy Kisner's poems have appeared in journals such as *Appalachian Journal, Pine, Mountain Sand & Gravel, Shelia-Na-Gig*, and *Spoon River Poetry Review*. Her poetry collections, *Inside the Horse's Eye* and *Last Days of an Old Dog*, are available from Finishing Line Press.

Marlene L'Abbé's art reflects the life she lives. She studied art in Montreal and currently lives in Athens. She exhibits paintings regionally and her art tiles under the name Waterspider Designs are available at Kindred Market, The Dairy Barn and at www.etsy.com/shop/tilemeastory. You can follow her on Instagram @waterpider3

Celia Lawren is the author of the poetry chapbook, *Among Dead Things*, published by Finishing Line Press in 2020. She retired from a successful marketing career in 2017 and lives in Knoxville, Tennessee, where she enjoys traveling the woods, rivers and valleys of East Tennessee.

Dana Malone grew up in Greenville, S.C., near Possum Kingdom. She lives in Nashville, where she sings, reads poems and tells stories (Tennessee Women's Theater Project, Bloom Stages, Poetry in the Brew, etc.). She has a chapbook forthcoming (Finishing Line Press) and won a 2021 poetry prize (April Gloaming Press).

Jessica Manack holds degrees from Hollins University and lives with her family in Pittsburgh, Pennsylvania. Her writing has recently appeared in *High Shelf Press, Prime Number Magazine* and *The Pittsburgh Post-Gazette*.

Born in eastern Tennessee and raised in southwestern Virginia**, Lonormi Manuel** has called Kentucky home for over thirty years. Her writing, both fiction and nonfiction, addresses universal themes in Appalachian settings. She writes not only about, but for the Appalachian people, and seeks to celebrate her homeplace through her work.

Jonie McIntire, author of *Semidomesticated* (Red Flag Poetry, 2021), *Beyond the Sidewalk* (Nightballet Press, 2017) and *Not All Who Are Lost Wander* (Finishing Line Press, 2016), is poetry editor at *Of Rust and Glass*, and hosts a monthly reading series called Uncloistered Poetry from Toledo, Ohio. Learn about her at https://www.joniemcintire.net.

Mimi Railey Merritt began a psychology major at Duke University, then changed her major to English. After grad school at UNC-Chapel Hill, she was a newspaper reporter in North Carolina and Virginia, a technical writer in Kentucky, and then a communications professor at Bluefield College in Virginia. She lives in West Virginia.

Barbara Marie Minney is a transgender woman, award-winning poet, writer, speaker, and quiet activist. Barbara is the author of *If There's No Heaven*, winner of the 2020 Poetry Is Life Book Award, and the Poetic Memoir Chapbook Challenge. Barbara lives in Tallmadge, Ohio. Follow her at www.barbaramarieminneypoetry.com.

Eileen Mouyard is a writer and baker currently living in Western North Carolina alongside her daughter, Clementine, and a lot of books. She is a third-generation writer behind her father and grand-father who have all lived, worked and sought inspiration amidst the pastoral landscape of Appalachia.

Corie Neumayer spent the early years of her life in the countryside of Rowan County Kentucky. With her family, she moved from the mountains to Louisville, where she attended college and became an art teacher. Now retired, she shows her work professionally in a Louisville gallery. She is still a child of the mountains of Appalachia.

Amy McCleese Nichols was the 2016 recipient of the University of Louisville Creative Writing Award for Poetry; her work appears in *Appalachian Review* and *Pine Mountain Sand and Gravel*. Originally from Flemingsburg, Kentucky, she holds a doctorate in Rhetoric and Composition from the University of Louisville and serves as Director of Writing Resources at Berea College.

Valerie Nieman's latest, *In the Lonely Backwater*, joins *To the Bones* and three earlier novels and three poetry collections, including *Leopard Lady: A Life in Verse*. A graduate of West Virginia University and Queens University of Charlotte, she is an NEA recipient and a former journalist and professor of creative writing.

Angela O'Curran-Lopez was born and raised in Southeastern Ohio. She graduated from Ohio University with a Bachelor of Science in Spanish. She is married with two children, ages 11 and 15. In addition to family, her interests include music, traveling, and researching genealogy. Angela is also passionate about writing and photography.

Eve Odom is a writer from Western North Carolina, who currently resides in Asheville, N.C. with her husband and son. She enjoys writing humorous, yet thoughtful, essays and is being published in the 2022 Spring Edition of *The North Carolina Literary Review*.

Elaine Fowler Palencia grew up in Morehead KY. She is the author of six books of fiction; four poetry chapbooks; a short monograph, *The Literary Heritage of Hindman Settlement School*; and a scholarly work, "On Rising Ground": The Life and Civil War Letters of John M. Douthit, 52nd Georgia Volunteer Infantry Regiment.

Frauke Palmer's studio is the out of doors. That's where she takes her pictures; that's where she finds her inspiration; that's where her ideas spring forth. Back home she sits in front of her computer and relives all those moments out in the desert hiking through the wide-open landscape learning about nature's ways.

Virginia Parfitt was born and raised in Western Pennsylvania. Much of her writing is informed by the rural landscape of northern Appalachia, the sounds and the scents, and the life and the death of the Earth. She nourishes these passions with words, written and spoken. She resides in southeastern Pennsylvania with her family.

Lisa Parker is a native Virginian, a poet, musician, and photographer. Her book, *This Gone Place*, won the 2010 Appalachian Studies Association Weatherford Award and her work is widely published in literary journals and anthologies. Her photography has been on exhibit in NYC and published in several arts journals and anthologies.

Tina Parker is the author of three books of poetry, most recently *Lock Her Up* published by Accents Publishing in 2021. Tina grew up in Bristol, VA, and she is a long-time Kentucky resident. To learn more about her work, visit www.tina-parker.org or follow her on Instagram @tetched_poet.

Chrissie Anderson Peters, a Southwestern Virginian native, now resides in Bristol, Tennessee. Her work has been published in *Still: The Journal, Pine Mountain Sand & Gravel*, and *Clinch Mountain Review*, and has placed in contests with Tennessee Mountain Writers, Inc. and the Mountain Heritage Lit Festival.

Lee Peterson has one full-length collection and many individual poems in the world. Her writing, and community interests center on issues of human rights, displacement and migration, motherhood, and the lived experiences of women and girls. She teaches at Penn State University's Altoona campus and lives in Central Pennsylvania.

Cat Pleska is an author, editor, and educator. Her memoir, *Riding on Comets,* was published in 2015 by WVU Press. Her essays and memoirs were published in *Still: The Journal, Change 7 Magazine*, and others. She teaches writing for Marshall University and is the president of Mountain State Press.

Susan Powers holds a BFA in Painting from Carnegie Mellon University with a minor in Creative Writing, and an MFA in painting from Pratt Institute. She is an Adjunct Lecturer in the department of Art at Carlow University. Visual perception, memory and the Appalachian environment influence her writing.

Bonnie Proudfoot moved to West Virginia in 1979, and currently resides in Athens, OH. She received a Fellowship for the Arts from the WV Department of Culture and History. She has published fiction and poetry. Her novel, *Goshen Road* (Swallow Press, 2020), was long listed for the PEN/ Hemingway award.

L. Renée is poet and writer from Columbus, Ohio. Her family migrated from West Virginia coal mines and Virginia tobacco farms. She holds an MFA from Indiana University, where she served as Nonfiction Editor of the *Indiana Review*. Her poems have been published in *Tin House Online, Poet Lore, the minnesota review, Sheila-Na-Gig Online* and elsewhere.

McKenna Revel is a poet from Mount Sterling, Kentucky. This is her third year with the Women of Appalachia Project.

Tonja Matney Reynolds resides in Ohio, but her parents are from southwest Virginia. Her work has appeared or is forthcoming in *Still: The Journal, Streetlight Magazine, 100 Word Story*, and elsewhere. Tonja's novel was longlisted for Regal House Publishing's 2020 Petrichor Prize for Finely Crafted Fiction. More at TonjaMatneyReynolds.com.

Barbara Lyghtel Rohrer comes from the river towns of Northern Kentucky; Norwood, Ohio; Pike County, Kentucky; Peebles, Ohio; rivers, creeks, hills and woods that shaped the houses, words and music of these communities, shaped her father, her mother, the man she lived with for eight years as wife. Their roots are my roots, never to be unentwined.

Barbara Sabol's latest poetry collection, *Imagine a Town*, was published by Sheila-Na-Gig Editions. Her poems have most recently appeared in *Evening Street Review, The Copperfield Review, One Art, Mezzo Cammin*, and *Modern Haiku*. Her awards include an Individual Excellence Award from the Ohio Arts Council. Barbara conducts poetry workshops through Lit Cleveland.

Shei Sanchez's writing can be found in *Gyroscope Review, Sheila-Na-Gig online, Entropy Magazine, Sepia Journal*, and other places. More of her work is forthcoming in *Golden Walkman Magazine, Pudding Magazine*, and Woodhall Press's anthology *Nonwhite and Woman*. She lives on a farm with her partner outside Athens, Ohio.

S. Renay Sander's love of the spoken word began amidst a family of storytellers in Tennessee. Her poetry and stories have appeared in several anthologies including, WOAP's, *Women Speak*. Her chapbook, *Dancing in Place*, was published by Nirala Publications in 2019. She writes from her home in the Cuyahoga Valley.

Susan Truxell Sauter's poems appear in *Apalachee Review, Voices from the Attic, Anthology of Appalachian Writers*, and Women of Appalachia Project: *Women Speak*; and in the anthologies *Nasty Women & Bad Hombres* and *Fracture: Essays, Poems, & Stories on Fracking in America*.

Roberta Schulz is a singer songwriter and poet originally from Grant's Lick, KY. Her latest chapbook, *Touchstones* (2020) is published by Finishing Line Press. Her poems have appeared in *Sheila-Na-Gig, Still: the Journal, Riparian, Kudzu*, and *Main Street Rag*. She writes songs on a mountain in NC.

Jeanne Shannon, Albuquerque, New Mexico, grew up near Wise, Virginia. Although she has lived in the west most of her adult life, to her, southwest Virginia is still "home." Her novella *The Sourwood Tree*, set in that part of Virginia, won a New Mexico Book Award in fiction in 2018.

Susan Sheppard's poems have won a number of awards including the Edgar

Allan Poe Memorial poetry prize and In Pittsburgh Award. Her work has appeared in *Yellow Medicine Literary Journal, Pierene's Fountain, Earth's Daughters, Fed from the Blade, 5AM, In Pittsburgh, Loblolly, Nimrod, Ohio Review, The Penn Review* to name a few. Sheppard is of Lenni-Lenape (Delaware), Shawnee and European ancestry and a descendant of some of West Virginia's earliest settlers as well as local Native American tribes. **Editor's note**: Susan was dear to us all and will be greatly missed. We are so grateful her words will live on.

Cynthia Shutts has been Appalachian all her life, though she moved in and out of the region often. She holds a Master of Arts in liberal studies from Hollins University and has had poetry appear in *Artemis, Cargoes, the album, the Roanoke Review, Pooka Review, Gambit* and others.

Sarah Smith is a board certified family physician and mother of two. She trained at Ohio University in Athens, Ohio. The inspiration for her poem was from interactions she had in medical school. She enjoys writing poetry in her spare time.

Anna Egan Smucker is the author of nine books, including *No Star Nights* (Knopf). A resident of Bridgeport, WV, her poems have been published in several anthologies and literary journals. Her first poetry chapbook, *Rowing Home*, a Semi-Finalist in their New Women's Voices Chapbook Competition, was published by Finishing Line Press in 2019. www.annasmucker.com

Lacy Snapp is pursuing an MFA at Vermont College of Fine Arts. Her debut chapbook, *Shadows on Wood,* is published by Finishing Line Press. She graduated with her MA in English from ETSU where she now teaches as an adjunct professor and works as a carpenter for her self-run business, Luna's Woodcraft.

Lois Spencer's publishing credits include *Ohio Teachers Write, Iris, Anthology of Appalachian Writers, The Poorhouse Rag*, and *Women Speak*. She earned two Ohio University degrees, BSEd and MSEd and her MALL at Marietta College. A memoir, *In the Language of My Country* (Outskirts Press 2017), highlights a uniquely Appalachian experience.

Anne Dyer Stuart was nominated for Best New Poets 2016 and won New South Journal's 2012 prose prize. Past publications include *AGNI, Cherry Tree, Raleigh Review, Third Coast, Sugar House Review, The Texas Review, Louisiana Literature, Fiction Southeast, New World Writing*, and *The Louisville Review*. She teaches at Bloomsburg University.

While pursuing her MFA at Southern Illinois University Carbondale, **Laura Sweeney** was awarded a residency at Sundress Publication's Firefly Farms, near Knoxville, Tennessee, which inspired a series of poems about Appalachia. Her poems and prose have been published in the States, Canada, Britain, and China. She facilitates "Writers for Life" in Iowa and Illinois.

Natalie Sypolt is the author of *The Sound of Holding Your Breath* and her work has appeared in *Glimmer Train, Appalachian Review, Still: The Journal*, and others. She is co-editor of *Change Seven Magazine* and works as an Associate Professor of English at Pierpont Community & Technical College.

Diane Tarantini grew up in Huntington, West Virginia, but now calls a 110-year-old Sears kit house in Morgantown, home. Tarantini is the communications director for a nonprofit that serves the women and teen girls of West Virginia and hustles sideways at social media management, freelance writing, and blogging.

Jessica D. Thompson's poetry has appeared in journals such as *Appalachian Heritage, Sows Ear*, and *Southern Review* in addition to numerous anthologies, including *Circe's Lament: Anthology of Wild Women Poetry* (Accents Publishing). Her ancestor, Abraham Raymer, was one of the earliest settlers to arrive in Kentucky.

Poet and author **Patricia Thrushart** has published three books, *Little Girl Against The Wall, Yin and Yang,* and *Sanctity: Poems from Northern Appalachia.* Her work appears regularly in The *Watershed Journal* and on the websites *Dark Horse Appalachia* and *North/South Appalachia.* Her poems have been published in *Tiny Seed, Tobeco* and *The Avocet.*

Beth Jane Toren is a founding member of the Poison River School of Poetry, a loosely knit group of poets from West Virginia. She presents creative writing as Ruby Meadowlark, Dixie McCall, R.N., and Granny Stretch-pants, and works as an academic librarian at West Virginia University in Morgantown, WV.

Elizabeth Tussey is a graduate of the NEOMFA Consortium and currently develops caregiver education materials for a hospice. Her work has appeared in *Barn Owl Review, Postcolonial Text, Silenced Press,* and *Uncommon Grackle.* She hails from Salem, Ohio but currently lives in Coraopolis, Pennsylvania.

Susan O'Dell Underwood directs the creative writing program at Carson-Newman University. Besides two chapbooks, she has one full-length collection of poetry, *The Book Of Awe* (Iris, 2018). Her novel *Genesis Road* is forthcoming in 2022 from Madville Publishing. Her work appears in a variety of journals, including *Oxford American, Ecotone,* and *Alaska Quarterly Review.*

Jayne Moore Waldrop is the author of *Retracing My Steps, Pandemic Lent: A Season in Poetry* (both from Finishing Line Press), and *Drowned Town* (University Press of Kentucky, 2021). She lives in Lexington, Kentucky.

Randi Ward is a poet, translator, lyricist, and photographer from Belleville, WV. She earned her MA in Cultural Studies from the University of the Faroe Islands and is a recipient of the American-Scandinavian Foundation's Nadia Christensen Prize. MadHat Press published Ward's second full-length poetry collection, *Whipstitches*, in 2016. www.randiward.com/about

Donna Weems sings at Pattifest, the Gardner Winter Festival, and the Osage Street Festival. She soloed for "Songs of Scott's Run" and is featured on the CD. She joined Al Anderson, raising over $20,000 for Ugandan orphans. She was a cast member of the folk operetta, "The Hobo's Homecoming."

Mary Beth Whitley was born and raised in Southern Ohio on a dirt road called Tick Ridge. Unrestricted hours playing in the woods and fields helped shape her values and aesthetics. Whitley creates artwork highlighting the Appalachian countryside through her unique process of combining digital c-prints with beeswax and pastels.

Karen Nelson Whittington lives on a small, SE Ohio farm. Her poetry or fiction have been published in past *Women Speak* anthologies, *Gyroscope Review, Anthology of Appalachian Writers* and *Pudding Magazine*. Three poems are forthcoming in the *Northern Appalachia Review*, Volume 2.

Sherrell Wigal comes from many generations of people living and working the land in Appalachia. With carefully chosen words, Sherrell encourages readers to move beyond their expectations. Her poems challenge and inspire. Sherrell's poetry has been published throughout the region and she conducts readings and workshops when asked.

Dana Wildsmith's newest collection of poetry is *One Light*, Texas Review Press. She's the author of a novel, *Jumping*, and a memoir *Back to Abnormal: Surviving with An Old Farm in the New South*. Wildsmith has served as Artist-in-Residence for Grand Canyon National Park and Everglades National Park.

Beth Wolfe is an educator, leader and communicator living in Scott Depot, West Virginia. A native Appalachian, her writing is as eclectic as her English and chemistry teaching background would suggest. Her house is full of jazz, thanks to her husband and dog hair, thanks to her Golden Retrievers.

CALL FOR FINE ART
DAIRY BARN ARTS CENTER EXHIBITION 2023

We believe that all women are capable, courageous, creative and inspired.

EXHIBITION DATES:
January 13, 2023 - March 12, 2023

AWARDS: Best of Show, First Time Participant, People's Choice and Three (3) Juror Awards

CALL FOR ENTRY:
Submissions Open: September 15, 2022
Submission Deadline: November 1, 2022

NOTIFICATION:
November 15, 2022

DELIVERY OF ACCEPTED FINE ART:
January 3-9, 2023

OPENING RECEPTION:
January 13, 2023

THE DAIRY BARN ARTS CENTER
www.dairybarn.org

www.womenofappalachia.com

Sheila-Na-Gig Editions

CPSIA information can be obtained
at www.ICGtesting.com
Printed in the USA
LVHW022123211221
706892LV00003B/8